It's Just Me

A woman's journey through
Poems, Prose, and Recipes

BARBARA MANN

With GOD all things are possible.
MATTHEW 19:26

authorHOUSE®

AuthorHouse™
1663 Liberty Drive
Bloomington, IN 47403
www.authorhouse.com
Phone: 1 (800) 839-8640

Published by AuthorHouse   04/30/2015

ISBN: 978-1-5049-0716-3 (sc)
ISBN: 978-1-5049-0715-6 (e)

Library of Congress Control Number: 2015905836

Scripture quotations marked KJV are from the Holy Bible, King James Version (Authorized Version). First published in 1611. Quoted from the KJV Classic Reference Bible, Copyright © 1983 by The Zondervan Corporation.

Print information available on the last page.

Any people depicted in stock imagery provided by Thinkstock are models, and such images are being used for illustrative purposes only. Certain stock imagery © Thinkstock.

This book is printed on acid-free paper.

This book is dedicated to so many that the list is endless. To everyone who gave me inspiration, hope, and strength, I thank you. My love for you is no less than the love for my family and friend listed below. So this book is dedicated to all of the people in my life, people that have made a difference and that I love dearly.

Renee, Darren, Ashley and Adrian Burrus

Kay, KC and Casey Nakamura

Charlie, Valorie, Rachael, Jeremy and Jerome Shires

Gloria Zahand

Some proceeds from this book will go to
Hatteras Island Cancer Foundation

CONTENTS

INTRODUCTION

We all have a journey to make.

This little book is the journey of a part of my life, a time of despair, hurt, love, need, and faith.

As you read, I hope you will connect, relate and maybe even carry away with you some small part, a small part that will aid you in a journey of your own.

I FOUND ME

I love myself for me now, not a reflection of
Who I thought someone wants me to be.

I can't live my life in someone's shadow trying
To please and loosing myself, my true being.

Love is sharing and caring, but being separate
To find your own true meaning in life.

The people that have touched my life
Have made me stronger.

I see their weaknesses, their strengths, their beliefs
And it has forged my own.

My faith has cast out my doubts.

"Love yourself as I love you", God said to me.
"When you accomplish this, the rest is easy."

There is something about having cancer that makes you want to run and hide. You put such a stigma on yourself for having had it. You have low self-esteem as if you have to hide your flaws and imperfections, ashamed of your body and how people may react to those imperfections. You feel embarrassed and have doubts about relationships. These feelings are experienced by both women and men.

There are so many reasons for hope and inspiration. Love for oneself is where it all begins. Love your body with its flaws, look in the mirror and see beauty, for you are beautiful inside and out. When you love yourself, others will love you as well. They will see that aura of light and beauty shining around you and want to be near you. Just remember, everyone has flaws, inside or out, cancer or not.

Let your light shine and someone will find you and your love.

JIM
The Beginning

I am no stranger to pain, suffering and loss. I have dealt with cancer since I was 24 years old.

We met on a blind date on my birthday and fell in love. Jim was just out of the Air Force and moved to Virginia from Mann's Harbor, a small community on the outer banks of North Carolina. We married within two years in the hot month of July. Two months later, two moles were found and both were cancer. One was on Jim's left shoulder and one on his lower back. Years of exposure to the sun while mating on his father's charter boat enraged the moles developing into Melanoma cancer.

Surgery was immediate. Large areas of flesh were scooped out where the moles were and skin was grafted from the top of his legs using a wood plane object causing great pain. After surgery, we were told Jim would eventually die from this; the cancer was already in his bloodstream. And so our struggle for Jim's survival began. We were so young and innocent and afraid. When treatments were suggested, we said yes. There were no advanced chemotherapy treatments for Melanoma, only experimental treatments and Jim suffered greatly from these. One doctor came from France. He used one inch squares of razor blades cutting into the skin under both arms and his groin near the lymph nodes after which he injected serum into the broken skin. After months of this, the skin was so inflamed the treatments were stopped. Next, radiated dead cancer cells were injected in his hip resulting in a dead skin hole the size of a pencil eraser. It never healed. And there were pills and injections and IV's. I was asked to keep check on any changes in moles, shape or color. Over the next few years, several were removed and tested. One near his spine proved to be cancer and Jim had his second surgery with skin grafts. New chemotherapy was developed by this time so Jim started monthly treatments spending a week each month in the hospital. After these were stopped, we actually had a few good years with no surgery or treatments. We were able to visit and spend time with Jim's young daughter, Renee and his loving family, Pop (James) and Mary, his parents and Joann and Crystal his sisters, in Mann's Harbor. We went fishing and boating and water skiing, enjoyed delicious fresh seafood dishes Mary and Pop would fix. These were happy times for us and we all knew these times together were precious moments, but how quickly things changed when the cancer demon reared its ugly head again. Having spread to each lung, back and shoulder and liver, we were left with only our prayers. After ten years of suffering experimental treatments, pills, injections, chemotherapy IV's and now radiation, I was losing him fast. I stayed with him at the hospital, slept in a chair by the bed holding his hand. He was afraid and could not breathe well from the cancer filled lungs. I thought I had felt all the hurt I could imagine until that Thursday I was asked to sign for a morphine drip to induce a coma and end his life in some form of peace. I went home to grieve. In my devastation, heart break, loneliness, I remembered our ten loving years together. And despite the hardships, I thanked God for giving me those ten years and the deep love we were able to share until the bitter end. Two days later, Saturday morning, I left the hospital early to shower and call Jim's family. I was home only 15 minutes when I received a call that Jim slipped away just after I left.

Jim died at age 36. I was 34. I buried Jim in the cold of February and went back to work to regain normalcy in my life. The house was empty and quiet and full of memories. Life would never be the same.

RENEE

Although Jim was gone, he left me one precious gift, Renee, his young daughter. I met her at age four. She was so cute and petite. She hated green peas and loved clog shoes. She was Jim's heart and how he loved her. She was only 16 when Jim died, a tender age for such heartbreak. The night after Jim's funeral, Renee slept with me. In the haziness of falling asleep, the room illuminated with bright light and I knew with all my heart Jim had come to be sure we were alright and say goodbye. Over the following years I watched Renee grow into a wonderful young woman, graduate and marry. So beautiful and not just on the outside, but beautiful on the inside. She gave me two wonderful and beautiful granddaughters, Ashley and Adrian. I watched as Ashley entered the world. All I could think was what Jim would think. I know he was watching and smiling and loving every moment. I know he still watches and loves.

A few years ago, I was visiting Renee and her family in North Carolina. I woke early that morning with the strangest feeling. Words flowed from my heart, my spirit. I grabbed a pen and paper and wrote down words, tears flowing. I went downstairs for coffee. I wanted to go outside to enjoy the peacefulness of Renee's lovely home and watch the sunrise. To my surprise, Renee was already up and outside. I sat beside her on the steps of the porch. I told her that her father was there watching over. I took the poem from my pocket and let her read. We both sat and cried together in the early morning knowing Jim would always be around.

WATCHING OVER

It comes to me in a dream.
It wakes me at night.
It fills my senses, sometimes with sadness, sometimes with delight.
Where did the time go? Why did you go?
Look what you left behind.

Are you there? Are you there watching over?

I treasure the thoughts of you.
I treasure every moment of your legacy.
They fill my heart with joy.
They make me feel loved as you did.
You live on. You live on in them.
And through them, I am still close to you.

You are there. Keep watching over.

When I visit, Renee pampers me with the undying unconditional love that is so prevalent in her being. The girls, Ashley and Adrian, shower Grandma B with love, hugs and kisses. How quickly they have grown into young women. Ashley graduated college May 2014 with a degree in Hotel Management and is now a Realtor as well and Adrian will graduate in a couple of years in Dentistry. Darren, Renee's husband, when he's not running their business, Cape Dredging, cooks wonderful fresh seafood and entertains us with boat rides to fish, clam and watch the sunset. He also makes me the best Bloody Mary. They're always letting me know I'm a part of their loving family.

Renee is a Realtor. She is also on the Board of the Hatteras Island Cancer Foundation. In twelve short years, the Foundation has raised one half million dollars in funds and returned it back to the very much needed community cancer patients. The Foundation funds help pay for treatments and prescriptions not covered by insurances. It also helps with transportation to and from the treatments. Please visit www.hicf.org to learn more about this small, but powerful Foundation.

Renee, Ashley and Adrian have inherited Jim's curse. They have moles all over their bodies. Some have been removed and tested, keeping watch for any sign of that dreaded disease. Living on the coast, it is hard to resist the ocean, sand, and fun. However, they are cautious of the sun's damaging rays.

I love them so much and pray for their long healthy life and happiness. I know their guardian angel still watches with love from above.

DAUGHTER

I never carried you in my body,
Never felt you kick or your heart beat.
But I watched you grow, you were so tiny and sweet.

I never birthed you, giving you breath and life.
But I have held you in my heart, in the depth of my sole,
Trying to keep you from strife.

You were his daughter, you became mine.
And I loved you then and will for all time.

I've watched you mature, watched you marry.
You gave me granddaughters, in my arms and heart to carry.

I love you daughter, God knows I do.
How much I cherish you in my heart, I will always try to show you.

I never remarried, although I might have one man. But life has a way of making decisions for me.

LLOYD

Jim was a finance manager and salesman in the automobile business. I worked in the accounting department for a firm that sold diesel test equipment worldwide. Our jobs were connected in the same industry. So when an opportunity presented itself to start a small business selling hubcaps, wheel covers and wheels, I dove right in. I did not know a thing about this business and my family and friends thought I had lost my mind. Looking back, I probably had. I was grabbing at straws to stay connected to Jim.

I had a very unique business lasting 23 years, unique that I was a woman competing in a "good ole boy" world. I really did not have any idea what the hell I was doing, but I had the strength, stubbornness and tenacity to try and make it work.

Lloyd was an auto wholesaler and was a friend of mine and Jim's for years. He was one of a few to have faith in me. He told me to just go for it and see what happens. He became somewhat of a permanent fixture around the shop, stopping by every day offering advice, help and knowledge. He convinced his salvage yard buddies to sell me loads of hubcaps and wheel covers acquiring many antique and collectible items. Living in the resort city of Virginia Beach, people came in my shop from all over, like Sweden, England, Germany, Canada, and around the US looking for wheel covers and hubcaps for their antique cars. This was just before the internet exploded, but we were shipping things all over. Life was good for a while. I was super busy working six days a week and long hours with help from some of my family. My brother, Charlie, worked for me for a while, three of my nephews and a niece as well. My father, having retired twice, came to work for me because he just wanted something to do. And "do" he did. He would bang dents out of the hubcaps (that was before they were made of plastic) and help install them. He would sing while he worked and customers would comment on his nice voice. Years later when he finally retired with the onset of dementia, my regular customers would always ask about him.

Lloyd was a little bit country and a little bit red neck and had a weird sense of humor that kept my spirits up, kept me laughing. Our friendship grew over the next couple of years and we eventually became lovers and fell in love. Life was comfortable. Some of our favorite times together after a long busy week were Sundays. We would just relax, snuggle in front of a fire, share some brandy and make love. Although Lloyd was 20 years older than me, our lovemaking was always passionate, tender and fulfilling. Lloyd loved NASCAR and football and fishing. He loved being out of doors. More than anything, Lloyd loved to hunt, especially deer. I hardly saw him from October until January. Every Saturday night he would bring home a cooler of fresh venison soaking in ice water, baking soda and vinegar to draw out the wild blood taste. When he cooked a roast, it tasted like beef. I bought him a meat grinder and we made venison sausage and ground meat for venison chili and burgers. We had so much fun. We were together five years when one day in October when he should be chasing rabbits or deer, he was diagnosed with colon cancer. It was devastating. Our world collapsed and went dark. Why? Why now? The night before he entered the hospital, we held each other, promising all would be ok. We would get through this and finish our life together. The next day, my birthday, he entered the hospital for surgery. The waiting room was full of family and friends. We all cried when the doctor took us to a private room and gave us the bad news. Cancer was everywhere and he would not live. The doctor had installed a colostomy to help his body function for as long as possible. As his illness progressed, I became his nurse and caregiver. I took care of his colostomy, changed his IV bag, flushed his permanent port and managed his morphine pain pump. I took him weekly for chemotherapy and radiation, but still the cancer consumed his frail body. One day sitting outside with Lloyd, he gave me an engagement ring and said, "I should have done this a long time ago". We cried but spoke no words for we both knew the ring was all there would ever be.

When pain got so bad and harder to control, he entered the hospital. His body was shutting down. His intestines were completely consumed by the cancer and the cancer had spread to vital organs. Within three days, I was asked to see the doctor privately. I was told to get a hospital bed for my home and asked if I knew what this meant. I said yes, he was being sent home to die. God why? My brain, heart and soul screamed! Why? Not again.

His family and I settled him in the hospital bed at home. He was almost comatose, but within two days, his pain was out of control. He was taken back to the hospital that evening. The next day was my birthday. One year from his surgery. He fought death and the pain. He refused to just slip away as Jim did. As the day and night went on and the pain medicine was constantly increased, he still fought. Soon I realized the time. I kissed him and whispered in his ear how much I loved him and couldn't bear to see him suffer anymore. I also whispered it was not my birthday anymore so don't stay any longer suffering. Go with the angels. Go to God. Around 3 am, he finally slipped away. I will never know why he endured such pain and suffering.

The mind is a wonderful machine, but the heart runs that machine.

WHY?

Is it wrong to ask why? Is this happening a must?
I've been told not to question, only trust.

When your life hangs by a thread, is it wrong to demand?
"Why me?" he asks, "Is it God's command?"

It is only human to want to know, to have an answer.
But suppose there is no answer.

Do we keep asking why?
Or do we simply trust and die?

After Lloyd's death, a friend gave me a plaque for the wall. It read, "When you get to the end of your rope, tie a knot and hold on". I had reached the end and tied the knot, but I was slipping.

Faith brought me back.

MY RESURRECTION

You found me, God, in the nick of time.
I was falling, falling.
I thought I had been abandoned in my hour of need.
I was in that place. You know it, you know where.
Between insanity and reality. Dangling.

With so little realness in life, I grasped and held tight.
Not knowing how vulnerable I was with my broken heart in my hand to give away.

So I put on a happy face for others to see,
While I soaked my pillow in tears at night and
Prayed for your everlasting strength and love.

All I had to do was ask, you gave it so freely.

My faith, my destiny was and is always in your hands.
Dear Lord, you shelter me and keep me safe.

I HAVE NO YESTERDAYS
TIME TOOK THEM AWAY
ALL I HAVE IS TODAY

I purchased a hand painted wall hanging in a small art gallery on the boardwalk in Ocean City, Maryland. Jim and I were on our honeymoon. I don't know why I bought it. I was just struck by the sadness of it at the time.

But is this true? No yesterdays? Over the years I have looked at this hanging on my wall. I have slowly come to realize how I feel about the verses. Most of us might say that time takes away hurt and pain, the memories we don't like to think about. Maybe that's true. I think we need some of those memories, hurtful, painful, just like our happy ones. I have so many happy memories that weave, intertwine, in and out the sad ones. I've finally learned that is all part of life.

Jim, Lloyd, Mom and Dad's deaths were hurtful and painful, but I have learned to look past that and look at their lives. They all lived. We live. They created memories as we are creating memories. We do have yesterdays, some of them, time has taken away. How sad. For loved ones like Dad with Alzheimer's, so many of his yesterdays were lost. I would sit with him and wonder how horrible and frightening it must be that he did not know me or the house we shared as a family. He was so fragile and scared. I wished he could have his yesterdays, could remember me one last time. He died alone, even though we were by his side.

Some say time heals all wounds and I believe that to be basically true. Time heals pain and hurt so we are able to have our yesterday memories. And as far as "All I Have Is Today", well we should certainly live in the moment and give from our hearts, compassion, love and understanding. Be helpful to those who can't help themselves. We are beacons of love.

I remember shortly after Jim died, a good friend was diagnosed with cancer and it progressed rapidly. In only a short time, she was near death. I visited her on a Saturday. Her sister told me she had given up. She wouldn't eat, wouldn't hold her baby boy, and was pushing everyone away. I sat with her and talked. After a while, she cried and told me she didn't want her family to love her because she was going to die and hurt them. I held and comforted her. Then I took her hands and looked in her sad eyes and told her how wrong she was. The only thing her husband, children and family had right then was to be able to love her and no matter what she did, they would still love her and want to be with her. I told her to hold her baby that he needed his mother's touch and kisses and smiles. Hug her children and family and tonight in bed, hold her husband and let him hold her. Give to them what they need from you and receive what you need from them. Love. We talked a little longer and she was smiling when I left. On the way home, I remembered how Jim had tried to withdraw from me, how we had made an agreement to always care and love each other forever.

A few weeks later, my friend died. Her sister told me that after I left her that day; she ate, washed, put on a pretty gown and her wig and a little lipstick. She held her children and we suspect, held her husband that night as well.

COME HOME

Come, Come. I know you are tired.
Come, Come. It is time to rest.

Come, Come. Don't be afraid and sad.
Come, Come. They will never forget.

Come, Come. They will always love.
Come, Come. I am waiting for you, my child, to come Home.

We have today to express love and compassion and we should not let it pass without doing so. I remember the day Mom died. She called every one of her children to say she loved them. It was three days before Christmas and she was baking cakes. The ones she baked every Christmas that we loved so much. I was so busy at work, I had to call her back. She said she was so tired. I asked her to just go and sit down and rest that my sister could finish the cake. She said she loved me. The last words I heard her say. She sat on the couch and died of a heart attack. She had given the gift of love to all of us before she died. She said she loved us.

This memory is painful but also loving. It's all woven together and I can't, I won't separate it. Live in the moment, make memories and don't let time take too many away. What we do today is a yesterday memory, tomorrow.

I hand made a Mother's Day card for Mom when I was in the first grade. I found it after Dad died in a box Mom called her Memory Box. I now have it in my memory box. It simply read,

BUTTERFLY HOVER NEAR MY MOTHER

TELL HER THAT I DEARLY LOVE HER

H

Two years I was alone again after Lloyd's death, healing, trying to find some sense of direction.

Believe me when I tell you that loneliness makes for strange bed fellows. Believe me even more when I tell you that there are worse things than being alone.

Working was healing. I didn't have much time to think except at night when I got home. The emptiness, aloneness crept in. I swore I wouldn't let anyone get close again. The hurt is too much, just too much.

I got calls from all over for items and one day a young fellow called from Newport News needing a Lincoln center cap for an aluminum wheel. He kept calling back wanting to talk but I always told him I was busy. One day I had just locked the shop door closing for the day when the phone rang. I don't know why I answered because the call would eventually lead to heartache. The young fellow wanted to know if I still had the Lincoln center and I told him yes. He wanted to talk, so we did. He was from the mid-west living in Virginia with family. He was working at a tire shop and said he was an auto mechanic. He was also 18 years younger than me. I told him I was old enough to be his mother and he told me he already had a mother. We laughed. He was quite funny. We met the next day when he came to pick up his center cap. He was goofy acting and sort of carefree. He asked me out on a date and I said no. He persisted for weeks and God only knows why, but I finally said yes. We had lunch and he said he had never seen the ocean. We went to the beach and walked the sand in the middle of January. He was a big kid and I knew he would be trouble. At this point in my life, I really didn't care. I took the plunge, just for fun I said and it was fun for a long time. His youthfulness and innocence was a bit refreshing. I knew I was making a mistake but, I needed the laughter and the freedom to just be me. My life was ok again for a while. I just did not see the next storm coming.

Mom had died and my sister continued to live with and help Dad. She began telling me about the strange things Dad was doing. He was increasingly getting lost while driving, driving on the wrong side of the road, forgetting who she was, sleeping in his chair all day, not eating, not bathing, to name a few. She asked me to help. I had always looked after Mom and Dad and their affairs. I was the executrix of their estate, keeping watch over their finances. When my sister said she needed help, I said yes. I knew the only way I could really help was to be there. I sold my home and moved back to my childhood home. My boyfriend was not too happy. He missed my garage with the pool table and a place to work on his car, missed the big house with the pool and hot tub, he missed our ability and freedom to just go when we wanted. You name it, he missed it. I had spoiled him and I had to admit that I missed my freedom in more ways than one. Three months after I moved in, my sister left. I couldn't blame her. She had been with Mom and Dad for a few years and my sister needed her own care and nurturing. Life was not easy and it was about to get worse.

Trying to run a business, coping with an angry boyfriend, my sister leaving, and seeing that Dad was taken care of was, what I thought at the time, the hardest thing ever in my life. Due to his condition when I moved in, Dad wasn't expected to live more than a year at most. Not! I changed his diet making him delicious soups and healthy meals he enjoyed. I exercised him taking him shopping with me and walking the neighborhood. I took him to the doctor. He blossomed like a crocus reaching for the sun through the snow. Dad got healthier, stronger, and meaner. My sister had left and I kicked out my boyfriend. He also got meaner and I knew it would not end well if he stayed. I was alone again, caring for Dad, trying to run a business, and trying to keep my sanity.

WORSE THINGS THAN BEING ALONE

The laughter is fading.
The sex is nauseating.
You cringe from a threatening blow.
You're afraid to say no.

There are worse things than being alone.

You long for peace and quiet.
You just want to stop the noise, stop the riot.
How did things get so crazy?
Making my thoughts seem hazy?
Oh to have solitude, to be able to think.
My God, I need another drink.

There are worse things than being alone.

Was it loneliness that led me here?
All those nights my pillow held a tear?
The longing of a gentle touch, a caress.
Oh how now I could care less.

When love turns to fear and dread,
Waiting for the demon to raise its ugly head,

There are worse things than being alone

DAD

At first I could leave Dad alone in the house, come home at lunch and feed him and bathe him, settling him in until dinner. Later on, he started walking the dog and getting lost. The day I took his car keys, we both sat on the porch and cried, he for his loss of independence and me for my loss of him. I finally started to understand the real situation. I researched Alzheimer's and realized I was in over my head. I took Dad to the doctor who confirmed my fears. Medications did not help. I found a facility that provided day care for Alzheimer's patients. I was up a 5 am, fed and dressed Dad dropped him off and picked him up after work. Peace of mind. The world was right again for a while. Dad's temper got him kicked out of two day cares. Distraught, I found a firm that sent ladies to the house to care for Dad. Yes, there were the usual challenges of bad care givers not doing their job, theft, but there were good care givers and with their help, we made it through. Dad's last care giver was sent from God. A wonderful African-American Christian woman, she took such good care of Dad and Dad was not easy to take care of. She was with me when he died. Seven years Dad lived. I joined the society of baby boomers taking care of their parents. I spent weekends preparing foods for the week. Dad's care giver had her hands full and cooking meals was not an option. I cleaned house, washed laundry, cut the grass, shoveled snow all in my spare time.

Time went by day after day, year after year. Dad's memory got worse, but his appetite stayed strong. He loved to eat and I cooked everything he loved. Since he was almost blind by this time, I would sit beside him and feed him. He would smack his lips and almost hum "oh that's good". Those are my joyful memories. You take the good with the bad. Life was tough and seven years of caring for Dad is enough to fill another book.

A LOST WORLD

I watch the face for any sign of recognition.
I listen to the rambling for a glimmer of hope.
He is in another place I cannot reach.
I love and care for him as he curses and strikes out.
What does he see? What is he thinking?
When he smiles, frowns, and reaches about?

Where you have gone, my father, I wonder.
To a lost world I cannot see.
You don't remember the present. You don't remember me.
The words "you're not my daughter", sting. I cry for love lost.
But I hope somewhere deep in this lost world, my face he can see and knows it's me.

He fades each day before my eyes. No amount of love can make it stop.
He falls deeper and deeper into his lost world.
This hard disease, this cold disease, this cruel disease, one I hope will someday cease.

I hold his hand, I nurture his body, I sing to his soul.
I wish for his happiness, his inner salvation.
And when his journey ends, I pray for his everlasting peace.

Dad passed away two weeks after suffering a stroke. I felt empty. All of a sudden, I had nothing to fill all my time. I tried to sleep all night, but after years of interrupted light sleeping, I could not. I was in an empty house again. The quiet closed in. Overweight, depressed, lonely, one night I lay in bed thinking about me, my life and realized just how much I had neglected myself.

Dad died April 2006. In May 2006, I was diagnosed with endometria cancer.

CRY IN THE NIGHT

I hear your cry in the dark.
I feel your pain within the beat of my heart.

It has made you undone, the loss, loneliness, despair.
It has taken you over the edge, close to beyond repair.

The fear consumes you, your senses blind.
Within the darkness, you scream aloud,
Your way out you're trying to find.

Losing your strength with every breath.
Wake up, wake up before the little death.

I struggle to wake hearing your call,
Catch me, catch me, before I fall.

I awaken searching for you, but the only thing I find,
The tears on the pillow are really mine.

ME

My world came crashing in. Just when I thought I would get my life back, there was a chance I would lose it. The days of not knowing were excruciating. I felt like every nerve in my body was screaming and no one could hear. I could hardly work, didn't eat, and didn't sleep. Then on the Friday of Memorial weekend, the call came. It was truly cancer and I would need surgery. I would be referred to an oncologist. Oh God! Oncology. Chemotherapy. That weekend was one of the longest and hardest times of my life. I spent it alone crying, feeling sorry for myself, talking to and cursing God. Why, why me? I'm a good person. Finally spent from crying, I came out of the fog trying to accept and decide just what I needed to do. I was not only a good person, I was strong and determined to get through this like I've gotten through all the other tough times in my life. Whatever God had in store for me, I would see it through. My gynecologist was the sweetest and kindest doctor. The day I left his office, he held me in his arms and let me cry. That was the last time I ever saw him. When I first met my oncologist, I was not happy. He did not seem compassionate to my needs or feelings. He wanted to schedule my surgery in two weeks. He was going on vacation out of the country. I told him to go. I needed at least 30 days to get my affairs in order. I had a small business and needed to see an attorney about legal matters. He kept insisting that waiting was not the thing to do and wanted to perform my surgery before he left for vacation. I insisted that waiting was just what I was going to do and I would see him after his vacation.

Surgery was scheduled for July 12, 2006.

I took care of my legal affairs, a will, power of attorney to keep the business running, and a medical power of attorney stating that I was not to be kept alive by machine if something awful should happen before, during or after surgery. I began researching my cancer, trying to find some alternative to surgery. After watching Jim and Lloyd suffer from their treatments, I had told my family I would never subject my body to chemotherapy and radiation. I began reading anything and everything about natural cures. Natural herbs were not new to me. I had been taking them for years trying not to contaminate my body with drugs that had so many side effects. So when a friend of mine suggested I go see an Herbalist in Norfolk, I went. The Herbalist suggested taking several Chinese herbs including anti-tumor, formulas to cleanse my body and blood, liver cleaners, and herbs to build my immune system. I had pretty much decided not to have surgery until I discussed it with my sister, Kay, in California. She cried. She said she understood what I was doing and why, but to please have the surgery and get the cancer out of my body. I eventually agreed. She said she would come to Virginia and help me after surgery. My brother, Charlie, would come from Florida to help my nephew keep the business going.

So with legal documents done, surgery date scheduled, Charlie and Kay coming to help and my natural cure going full force, I had time to settle back and just think about the future. A future that was questionable if I let myself dwell on that possibility. I had to endure, I had to be strong. I would live through this. God has more plans for me I kept telling myself. I had Renee and two granddaughters. I wanted to see Ashley and Adrian graduate, go to college, marry and have children of their own. So much to live for.

So I did not think of the possibility of dying only the fact that I would live.

P AND ME

In my business, I spoke with so many people while taking orders or placing orders and so on, almost never meeting any of them. One nice man who worked in a body shop was going through a nasty divorce. He was angry and sad and had many problems. I would listen while he vented, silently praying that he could have some peace. I never mentioned my problem even though we had become phone buddies for months. One day he decided to visit and meet me. He rode up on his Harley. OMG! Tall, dark hair, great smile, handsome, Italian and 12 years younger than me. That combination would get any girls heart, and other body parts, pumping. Our talks were still mostly about his divorce situation, but much lighter. We laughed a lot now. We become real friends. So you can understand the disappointment, shock and hurt he felt the day before my surgery when I finally told him. He felt terrible for going on about his divorce when I never shared my illness with him. He asked which hospital and said he would visit. The next morning Sis, Charlie and I checked in and I had my surgery. I woke in my room alone. A nurse came in to check me and said my family would be in soon now that I was awake. A few minutes later in walks P with card in hand. He kissed my cheek. All that was going through my mind was how much I wanted this guy. It must have been the drugs that caused all those fantasies!

My sis stayed two weeks helping me recover. She took me for my visit to the oncologist. While my staples were being removed, I mentioned to the doctor that my left leg at the top near my groin was numb. All he said was that I would get used to it. Kay and I looked at each other in horror. Not so much that the surgery had probably caused the nerve damage, but the awful, no feeling, callus way he said it before he walked out the door. The numbness is still there and, nope, I never have gotten used to it. If that wasn't bad enough, his office manners were even worse. Never once did he ask how I felt. As soon as we sat, he immediately said he removed thirty some lymph nodes and eight had cancer cell activity. He wanted me to start chemotherapy the following week, every other week for three months. Sis held my hand and cried. He looked like a cold fish, no compassion in those eyes staring at me as he said I would not live without it. He took us to the chemotherapy area and turned us over to a nurse who proceeded to explain what my sessions would be like. I already knew, having lost my husband Jim and boyfriend Lloyd to cancer. I watched the suffering, the debilitation, and the lack of quality of life while they struggled to stay alive believing they would live. Their poor bodies raked with nausea and zapped of strength. Oh yes, I knew just what was in store. The appointment was set up for the following Tuesday.

As Sis and I left the office building and walked to the car, I said to her, you know I'm not doing chemo. It will kill me. I've told everyone since Jim died, I would never do it. With tears in her eyes, she said she knew I would say that. I told her I had to build my body up, not tear it down, and I needed to see my Herbalist. Now this is where I need to explain to you that this was **my** choice how to deal with **my** cancer. I'm not saying do as I have done. You must make your own decisions with your doctor as to how you want to treat **your** cancer. Since I started my herbal treatment in 2006, I have learned that major cancer treatment centers use natural treatments along with chemotherapy. Please research, research, research. I still do. We went the next day and updated my Herbalist on what had happened and he suggested the new herbs I needed.

The next day, I cancelled my chemo appointment.

Kay left on Sunday and my brother, Charlie, stayed another week until I could go back to work. I can never repay either for what they did to help. Leaving their jobs and families was a big sacrifice, a big testament of their love for me. The night before Charlie left, the incision in my navel broke open and "stuff" poured out. It was the hot month of August, but when I went to bed I shivered uncontrollably and prayed to God to let me live. I never told Charlie and as soon as I took him to the airport, I visited my Herbalist. When I explained what had happened and showed him my navel, he was happy. I was confused. He said it was great that my body was able to get rid of the toxic waste from the surgery. It was a cleansing and my body would not have to dispose of it. I felt better and was no longer afraid. I trusted him with my life and still do today. I went back to work, not able to do any heavy lifting and not able even today. Everyone said it would take a year to heal, but the swelling on my right side just wasn't going away. I faithfully took all my herbs and constantly researched the internet for anything new. I tried other natural things when what I read made since to my situation. After a few weeks, I was asked to come see my oncologist. His desk side manner was still pretty awful. He asked why I refused the chemotherapy that it is what he would have his sister do. I told him I wanted to live and the chemo would kill me. He told me without it, I would die in a year and a half with excruciating pain. Staring at each other, I asked if I should sign a release. He said no I may leave. As I walked out the doors of the building into the parking lot, I shouted for all to hear.

"I'm not gonna die!"

After a few days, my gynecologist called to ask why I didn't have the chemotherapy, my oncologist had called him. I explained my feelings and he said he respected my decision but felt I was wrong. Before we finished our conversation, I told him what the oncologist had said about dying in a year and a half with excruciation pain. Dead silence. Finally he said he was sorry that was said and to please call him if I needed. Life went on. I was healing and getting stronger, but my right side was still more swollen than the left. It was much later I discovered that my intestines were all located on my right side. Just thrown in and sewn up was how I felt. Was this why the oncologist was so sure to pronounce me dead in a year and a half? People have asked me why I didn't sue. I tried. I was actually told by an attorney he would not handle the lawsuit because his family might need medical attention from those doctors. Well good luck with that! I worked the best I could, lifting and doing all the things I shouldn't have just to keep the business going. I was deformed and over the years because of this, I have developed varicose veins. I have to monitor how long I sit. Long plane rides are hazardous to me for fear of blood clots. I walk to keep the blood flowing and the nerves in my left leg are still numb. I began to feel unattractive, that no man would ever want to hold me, look in my eyes and make love to me again. It haunted me every night alone in my bed. The other thing that haunted me was the words of the oncologist. "You will die in a year and a half with excruciating pain." It was always there in the back of my mind. I prayed and had long talks with God. I took my herbs without fail but the fear of dying lingered right on the edge of my whole being.

FEAR

It flows through me like a wave of dread carried by darkness.
It creeps in and consumes my consciousness.
I tremble and shiver with awareness uncontrolled.
If fear takes over it will bring destruction of my being, my senses, and my soul.

I must not fear for God is my salvation, to fear is not to believe.
I must keep my faith in all my thoughts, I will not be deceived.
I am his child and made in his image of perfection.
I will reject my fear, hold strong and have faith in God and his protection.

I continued struggling with work, health and faith. I was very fragile at this point. I could rely on the strength of my faith, but the strength of my body began to fail me. I could not lift 40 to 50 pounds anymore without feeling pain. Simple tasks became exhausting. It was becoming evident I needed to think about selling or closing my business. My brother and his family wanted me to move to Florida and live with them. With the possibility and fear of dying alone, I began preparing for the inevitable. P and I talked almost every day during work. He had made it to mediation in his divorce but had to vacate his home every other weekend until the divorce was final leaving Friday and returning Sunday night. On one of those evenings after mediation we spoke and I could tell it didn't go very well. I invited him to my house. We loved sitting on the back porch having a glass of wine, sharing a cigar. We talked for hours about our lives growing up, family and friends, hopes and dreams. This particular night I invited him to my bed. We made love for hours. He made me feel whole again, made me feel I was desired as a woman again. Holding me in his arms and looking in my eyes, he said I set him free from all the ugliness he had been living with lately. I thought about this after he left and realized what he had done for me.

SET FREE

At what point did the cage door open?
The door you put on your heart.
You slammed it shut to hold everything out,
Afraid to feel, afraid to hurt.
Love is the key to reopen your soul,
To be able to love again, feel again, to experience life again.
You said I set you free.
Did I set you free or did you me?

P stayed with me every other weekend and would visit me a couple of times during the week early in the morning. We made love, had coffee and breakfast and went off to work. Life was good again. P finally got a great job, his divorce and his own home to share with his children. I was happy for him although my heart broke when he moved into his new home. It marked a new beginning for his life, but an ending for us. P had his children one week and worked long hours the next and had very little free time. We saw each other some but I was pretty much alone. Life sucked again, but I had my memories, and I'll always remember P, our friendship, long talks, and yes of course, our early morning love.

STOLEN MOMENTS

You come to me in the early morning light.
You wrap your arms around me like wings of an angel and heaven truly descends.
Your love is tender and I am raptured as I surrender to your embrace.
The world around me explodes with passion and joy.
You gently kiss me leaving me lighthearted and breathless.
I lay wanting more, more of what's lingering in the depth of my being.
Until the next early morning light.

REMEMBERANCE and ENDING

I put Dads house and my business up for sale. The house sold and I moved into my little shop with my two small dogs for a few months until I went to Florida. I was homeless and the shop was not the safest place at night. I had no hot water for showers, but made do with a camping water bag that I filled with hot water from the water cooler. I had a refrigerator, microwave, toaster oven, hot plate, and electric skillet. I adapted and improvised. I tried not to think about the situation. I kept busy preparing for closing and the move. Lots of paperwork, selling stock, cleaning and lots of being alone. I would lie in my blowup bed at night and think about my life and wonder why God wanted me to live, what he had in store for me. I would think about the people who had come to my shop. The twenty three years I was open, many different people came through that door. I was never robbed or harmed in any way. I did have my share of strange customers, but in twenty three years not too many crazy things happened. The best things I remember were the people I could help, husbands or wives who had lost their spouse and cried out in loneliness and despair. Mothers, daughters, fathers, sons, brothers, sisters would talk and hug and share. The people with cancer I gave hope to and the hope they gave me. I shared my life and they theirs. One little lady with an oxygen tank and her husband came to my shop soon after having a radiation treatment. I sat her on a stool and we three talked very openly about cancer. I told them about my herbalist and my experience. A few weeks later when I visited my herbalist, this little lady and her husband were just leaving. Her husband smiled at me and pointed out the fact she was not using her oxygen tank. She hugged me and smiled. I never saw her again and I don't know the outcome but any quality of life is a wonderful gift. I was sad leaving my little shop. I have so many good memories of customers and business associates becoming great friends, memories of my nephew's daughter, who would stay with me at the shop. It had been my life for many years and my home for a few short months but it was time to move. A few weeks before I was to leave for Florida, I left my shop for good. I with my two little dogs went to stay with friends. They were neighbors down the street from my childhood home. The home in which my parents lived for 48 years and died, the home of my childhood memories, memories of Christmas and Mom baking, memories of my sisters and brothers, memories of Dad helping me with school projects and Mom teaching me to cook, memories of Dad and our years together as he slowly lost his own memories, memories, so many.

I laughed, cried, hurt and finally said good bye.

W

While staying with my friends, I met W. We were having dinner and W stopped by to talk about his 57 Chevy my friend was fixing for him. My friend was the neighborhood mechanic when he was not on a Navy ship. W and I became friends and spent some time together before I left. We went to dinner and to the beach, Virginia Beach, to talk and people watch. We would sit by the ocean watching the boats come and go. W loved sailing and I enjoyed it as well when we sailed together. This was a happy two weeks for us both, but it had to end. The two weeks passed by very quickly and it was time to say good bye. My brother arrived and a few days later we were on our way to Florida. W and I kept in touch, talking almost every day. He was my rock through times of stress, sadness and depression. His soft voice was the sound of encouragement as he kindly listened and asked how my day was. He soon took a job in northern Virginia, and I flew up to visit. This was the beginning of a four year long distance romance. We had fun and enjoyed our times together. Our passion cemented our friendship. Though the words were never spoken, our hearts knew we both loved and cared. W visited me in Florida and we went to Clearwater and St. Pete on the Gulf, the Keys, enjoying sailing and the sunsets. I visited him as he relocated from Virginia. I will never forget one time I flew to visit for New Year's Eve when there was snow and an ice storm. W suggested we go out for dinner. I told him he was crazy. For one thing it was dangerous and another I was freezing, having gotten used to the Florida heat. We decided to stay in. I made chocolate covered strawberries and we had champagne. It was a romantic night and W kept me warm. We even stayed close for a while after I moved to California. W flew in for a sales meeting and we went to San Francisco and the wine country. I finally got to take a hot air balloon ride. It was so wonderful. I felt so close to God floating around in the silent morning mist. Our short times together were exciting, fun and loving, but eventually the long distance and the three hour time difference took its toll. It was difficult coordinating time to talk in between his work and my obligations. So he ended the relationship. Just before this happened, W was diagnosed with prostate cancer. My heart broke. We were on Skype when his doctor called. I cried. He was alone like I was when I found out, alone and afraid. He asked for my help and I suggested an herbal formula I have been taking for years and I suggested foods that combat cancer. A few weeks later he called to say hi, he missed me and that he loved me. After several months, he let me know his prostate was on the mend with all levels back to normal. I'm so happy for him and his good news. I wish W all the happiness in life. I will always remember our times together with lots of smiles and love. In a book I read, the hero was sad sending someone away that he loved. He knew it would be best for her and protect her. They both accepted their fate, to love and be apart. After she left, he said it was better to have had ten days of love than years of regretting. How true.

I let my heart love for however long it last because it is better than the wondering and longing and regret of not letting love in.

MY SOUL

My soul is lighter now, the hunger is gone.
The need that was so strong has started to subside.
The mind and heart play tricks on you.
So be careful of their games.
For once you love and twice you hurt, you will never be the same.
If you are so lucky to find true love in your life,
What a blessing that would be.
People will change, the heart will change,
But only love can set you free.

MY NEW HOME

Leaving Virginia, Renee and my granddaughters, friends and family, my home, was sad for me, but Charlie and I took the long ride to my new home. We arrived to hugs and kisses and tears of joy. I finally began to feel safe, to be with family just in case something horrible happened. That night I slept sound for the first time in many years. I began to relax and started putting my life back in order. Charlie's wife, Valorie and I began unpacking and getting my room set. My two little dogs and I were happy. This was July 2008. I was two years cancer free, six months longer than what the doctor said I would live. How blessed I felt being with family and sharing their lives. My niece, Rachael, has a little baby boy, Jerome. He and I fell in love. Everyone said I, Auntie, was his favorite toy. He would say Auntie let's go in your room and play. We would watch videos and eat popcorn in my bed and he would want to sleep with me. The first time I said yes I couldn't sleep afraid I would roll on him and hurt him.

BLESS THIS CHILD

Dear God, bless this child who sleeps in my bed.
Watch over him from toe to head.
For his heart is pure and his spirit is free.
Take care of us dear Lord.
Little Jerome and Auntie.

When Charlie and I left, we drove home in a moving van full of my possessions. I had storage units to sort through and Valorie and I spent days unpacking and repacking boxes bringing things over to the house. The heat and humidity was horrible but we managed to scale down the boxes. We would curse and fuss about all the junk I had as we unpacked so many memories. It was really hard to get rid of those but having storage units was a financial drain. I finally got it down to one. The things that remained I could not bear to part with. Charlie works nights most of the time working until 4 or 5 o'clock in the morning. This type of work takes its toll on his body, but he endures to take care of his family. Because he sleeps most of the day, Val and I would go out shopping or to lunch and sometimes take the baby with us. That was always a riot and sometimes a challenge because he would run through the stores, laughing, and try to hide from us. Talk about heart attacks. Mostly, we had fun times. I of course was told I spoiled him. Yep, I did. Guilty. Charlie, Valorie, Rachael, Jeremy and Jerome are a loving family and I became a part of it. On the weekends we would swim and play in the pool with Jerome. Friends came over and we would cook and have a great time. I was so happy just to be alive and able to enjoy my new life with a family I love and that loves me. Charlie is a good cook and loves to cook as much as I do. We would both try new things, but I was the one who got blamed for making everyone fat! Oh well, guilty again. Charlie's dream is to one day open a small restaurant. I would love to see that happen and even be a part of it. I think it would be a lot of work but so much fun. They have just moved to the coast from Orlando area. We all love the beach and ocean, fishing and shrimping and crabbing. Fresh seafood is the best. Jeremy loves to surf and says he will one day come visit me and surf the west coast waters. Rachael works hard during the day and goes to school at night working on her degree in the health care field. And Valorie is the glue of the family keeping things together making sure everyone has what they need, especially Charlie and the baby, Jerome, even though she often neglects herself doing all the things she does for everyone. She's a good wife, mom, grandmother, and my friend. I love and miss them all dearly.

FAMILY

It's the bond that holds lives together.
It's the happy, the sad, the misunderstanding, and the stormy weather.
It's the love, the caring, the hopes, the dreams, and the sharing.

It's the loss and gain of life,
A family member, brother, sister, son, daughter, husband, or a wife.
It's the memories, sharing old ones and making new ones.

It's help in a time of need, kindness so great it makes the heart bleed.
It's the feeling of helplessness and the joy of forgiveness.

Put it all in a bag, shake it up and pour it out.
Blood is thicker than water, that's what life is about.

Family
Let us never forget who we are, where we came from, and where we are going.

Family
Always, always cherish.

Charlie and his family loving me and making me a part of their family was one of my greatest gifts.

God always knows when I need something or someone in my life. He sent me an angel to be my friend, giving me strength when there was weakness, hope when there was despair and faith when there was doubt. God sent Gloria.

GLORIA

One hot day, I was looking for something in my storage unit. A very nice lady drove up across from me to work in her unit. She walked over and asked if I needed any help. She said her mother was getting old and needed looking after and she was moving in with her. We talked about my journey with Dad and the one Gloria was just starting with her mother. We talked for a long time and she asked if I would like to go to church. I wrote down her phone number and before she left, we prayed together asking God for strength to complete our journeys. I felt she was a friend immediately although it was over two months before I called. Since I did not know my way, she picked me up and I felt God's love all around. Gloria is a true Christian, a very special caring person and I love her. She is so kind and spiritual, uplifting and encouraging. After service we sat in the church cafeteria and talked and shared some of our lives. Each week, I would join her for service, we would have lunch and talk and Gloria would go to work. It is amazing how bad you think your life has been until you talk to someone about theirs. That old saying walk a mile in my shoes is so true. Gloria was sent from God to bring me to that church. The peace I felt walking in was like a tonic. I would get there early so I could sit quietly and talk with God and thank him for my life. I often asked what he wanted me to do with my life and I knew one day he would answer. Gloria works at a rescue mission and helps so many people. The love she gives out is so incredible and never asks or expects anything in return. She truly does God's work. Gloria and I are still friends. We don't talk as much as we did but every now and then we catch up on what's going on in our lives.

I miss our chats and the laughter and tears we shared. I miss her friendship.

GLORY, GLORIA, HALLELUJA

She walks the straight and narrow though it is not an easy task.
She loves God and Jesus and it shows, there is never a need to ask.
Her life has been and is filled with troubles.
But she will be rewarded as goodness from God will surely double.

She cares with a huge heart, arms always open wide.
She will walk with you through hells damning fires ever by your side.
I love this dear lady, so full of spirit and life.
A true friend she is and I pray God eases her soul of any strife.

She walks with God and walks with me.
Why I cherish her friendship is so plain to see.
There is comfort from her grace and peace from her smile.
I pray silently she will be my friend forever as we chat and sit together for a while.

MY LITTLE ONES

I had settled in but after a while, my depression grew and self-worth diminished. I woke up one day and decided I needed a job. I needed to work and I needed to keep busy. I thought about my abilities. I was smart, still healthy and good with people. And then I thought about Dad and his Alzheimer's. He was old and helpless, fragile and needy. I found a local elderly care agency that helped the elderly with cooking, doctor appointments, shopping and other small needs. I interviewed and got a part-time job. I was trained in CPR and other minor medical necessities. I loved it. They say that music is the universal language. I say good food cooked with love surely is the universal smile maker. I cooked good nourishing food for my clients, made sure they were safe, clean. I took them shopping or did their shopping. I took them to visit friends and family or to doctor appointments. I loved taking care of them all. Some were angry, like Dad, for losing their independence, but after a while we became friends and they appreciated all my help and care. I was offered a cooking position for a lovely elderly couple. Cooking I soon found was only one of their needs. The lady of the house had the onset of dementia and had forgotten how to safely cook or operate the washer and dryer. So I was more than glad to do laundry and some housework along with the cooking. I went two days each week. I prepared meals to last until the next day I came. Some mornings I would fix a big hearty breakfast. It was like a celebration for them. The smiles and gratitude were heartwarming. I washed and styled hair occasionally and even washed the dog. The appreciation I was given was worth more than gold. My heart was filled up. One favorite client was a retired school teacher. She did not have dementia but had other illnesses. We became very good friends. She was so sweet. We went shopping, to doctor appointments, to visit family and friends. She was kind and I loved her very much. Another special client did have dementia and lived with a daughter. I would arrive at 7:30 in the morning and stay until 5:30 when the daughter came home from work. I would get her out of bed, bathe her, dress her and fix her breakfast. She loved blueberry pancakes. She loved to eat and I cooked her some very special food. I loved to see her happy. I was her caregiver for quite some time. I watched the slow progression of the disease as the months passed. She would talk to someone from her past and when I asked about it, I was told someone very young she loved had died.

FAR, FAR AWAY

I see your big bright eyes. I see you smile.
Where are you? What are you remembering?
A happy time, a happy place?

You talk to someone I cannot see.

Do I remember him, you ask. I don't I say.
Sadness starts to creep in. Oh yes! Now I remember him.
A smile lights up your face.

You chat about a time long ago, a place far, far away.
I cannot understand all,
But I hear you scold a child and send him out to play.

Your family says a child died young
And you talk to him each day and night.
It is surely my strong belief that angels keep us in their sight.

You are watched over and loved while he awaits
Your arrival in that place far, far away.

And as I sit beside you listening, I pray.
That someone will watch over me someday,
From that place far, far away.

I was feeling good about my life again. I was finally giving back. Little by little I understood God's plan. We are here to do God's work, to give and share, to give of ourselves, to help and care for one another, to love one another. I don't know why I got cancer, but I know what it feels like to be afraid, afraid of dying, afraid of being alone and dying. God gave me a second chance and I wanted to give thanks by helping others. It's our true purpose here to help our fellow man. I smile at people, say hello, ask how they are because everyone is important to me especially children and the elderly. They are so small and frail and needy. I call them my little ones.

MY LITTLE ONES

So frail, so hungry for attention, their eyes wide with anticipation for a kind word, kind gesture.
In their little world, miles away, each day a new adventure.

They may never remember your name,
But the expression of delight when they see your face is always the same.
So honest, true to themselves, ready for a fun game.

They are so small but their needs are so great.
Childlike, trusting, making your heart ache.

That smile, that hug, the gratitude,
Makes your heart break when you walk away.
Should I have done more, what if, if only I could?

ANOTHER NEW LIFE

I suppose you are wondering how I got to California and why I left friends and family in Florida. It was not an easy decision. I still have guilt leaving my brother and his family. I love them and miss them but I think California is my destiny. **I'm a foodie!** I have always loved to cook. Cooking is and will always be my passion. Before Jim's cancer came back the last time, I had just started a small catering business while working full time doing accounting. I did a wedding reception for someone who worked at Old Dominion University and she asked me to teach an evening class for Holiday Entertaining. I was only 33 years old. After the first class at ODU, I invited the ladies to my beautiful home in Virginia Beach to complete the course. We had so much fun and I have to admit I spent more than I was paid, but it was worth every penny. It was such a success, I was asked to continue. Unfortunately, this was the time Jim's cancer reoccurred and would soon end his life. So with all that being said and you have already read about my life after Jim's death, when my sister, Kay, called from California and told me that my nephew, Casey, and his friend, Scott, wanted to start a business making salsa, I was ecstatic. Over twenty years ago, I had gotten a pepper recipe. Over the years I have adapted the recipe, adding different peppers and other ingredients and spices making it into a salsa. I shared it with family and friends and to my surprise everyone loved it, especially Casey and Scott. I dreamed for years about starting a business. So even though it was a hard decision to leave Florida, it was the only decision to make to be able to start my salsa business. So I moved to California and a new adventure, a new chapter in my life began. Casey and Scott are young entrepreneurs, smart and worldly for their young ages with Master degrees and businesses of their own while working full time jobs. Casey has his own videography business while Scott is working on his PHD and teaching, both in their mid-twenties. That was November 2011. We started working on our business the following February 2012. I gave the boys the name I wanted for our business and they wanted to change it. I already had a slogan and they liked it. I gave them the story line for our video and they tweaked it. I drew a sample of what I wanted on the story board and production of our video began. After a couple battles of the ages, I won. Our business name is Dragon's Breath Salsa, our slogan is "Open a Jar and Share the Heat!", and our video is strong and fun, not too cartoonish. Soon we applied for trademarks. I had no idea this was such a long process and would cost so much. Casey and Scott have invested greatly. It took us over a year to get all three, name, slogan, and label. While we were working on the trademarks, I worked on developing other products with our salsa. We now have an original hot, original hotter, crushed hot, crushed hotter, a hot sauce still in progress, because the guys want it, YES!, hotter; a dry rub still in progress and a few other things still in thought process. Just recently we have obtained our insurance, sellers permit, our federal identification number, our LLC certification and I have a food manager's certificate and sis and I have a food handler's certificate. We are now looking at a manufacturer to bottle and label our product. My dream is so close to coming true, but there is more work to be done before it is realized and more money is needed to finalize the manufacturing process.

While waiting for things to happen, I have had time for reflection and to write this book. This past July 2014, I have been eight years cancer free. I don't think I would be here if not for the help and love of my family. The sacrifices Kay and Charlie made when I had my surgery, Charlie taking me in to live with him and his family, Kay bringing me to California to live with her, KC her husband, and Casey. I love my sis and her family. Like Charlie, Sis and I have been best friends all our lives. We have always given support to each other through the good and hard times. She is so smart and creative. Even though she has a stressful full time job, she has her own business in which she designs and creates beautiful jewelry. Together we do creative things like ceramics, hand paint and decorate birdhouses and wind chimes to make them all one of a kind, just to name a few. She laughs at me and says I'm weird but I think I'm just different! It's just me. We have fun together, help and nurture each other. I cannot stress enough the importance of family, the glue of life.

GODS WORK

God still has work for me and that part of my life is unfolding with this book. I am still meeting new people with stories of cancer. Lives touching lives. I walk to keep healthy and one day while walking, I stopped to pick some leaves and gumballs off a tree for a birdhouse I was painting. The owner walked out and I laughed and said he caught me stealing leaves. We immediately became friends and laughed and talked. As time went by and I would see him on my walks, I learned that his wife had had breast cancer and he said it almost killed him when he thought he would lose her. The hurt and pain and love in his eyes was very evident. Over the next months we shared stories. I shared my story of Jim and my salsa and he told me he made barbeque sauce. He gave me some of the sauce to try and it was so good, just like the Carolina sauce I enjoyed on the east coast. He tried and said my salsa wasn't hot enough! OMG! WT! He sounded just like Casey and Scott wanting me to make it hotter. Men, go figure. In my ceramics class, a gentleman shared with me his wife's cancer struggles and a teacher shared her triumph over breast cancer. Jim's sister Crystal lost her husband to cancer. A cancer he had battled for a number of years. My heart hurts for her for I know the struggles they both endured. Crystal is such a sweet and strong person having had cancer herself. I know God gives her strength and watches over. And a lovely, spiritual woman I met in the cosmetic section of Walmart one week before Christmas. We were both looking for a fountain of youth serum, LOL and she began telling me about her two battles with breast cancer, mastectomies and a very funny story of her reconstructive tweaks. She was so positive and up lifting, I shared a brief moment of my story and told her about this book. Christmas is such a wonderful time of year and to share our stories in the middle of Walmart was truly a spiritual experience. And yet Christmas Eve 2013, I received a Christmas card from Mark, the husband of my dear friend, Sherrill, in Virginia. She suffered for over a year with lung cancer and passed away in November. She was my friend for over 25 years. She was so happy that I was finally getting my salsa business going. She loved my salsa. She is truly missed. Her kind and gentle spirit touched my heart and will always be a part of it.

I know there will be many more. So many, but listening to them I keep seeing and hearing the stories of compassion, hurt and hope, devastation and triumph, suffering and healing, anger and love, death and survival. There is hope for all of us.

We will beat this demon one day and while we are fighting we will connect and give strength to each other for we will all become **VICTORS**, victims of cancer, survivors.

Recently a friend said that life is too short to be embarrassed or say you're sorry. I thought about this and agree that life can be too short, but never miss an opportunity to let someone know how you feel, to say you're sorry, to say you care, to say you love. You may not get another opportunity. So as you sit reading this little book, try to remember you have yesterday and today and, yes, tomorrow. Allow yourself to remember the good and the bad.

Cry if you need to cry, scream if you need to scream, heal if you need to heal, and laugh if you need to laugh. Go out and hug someone.

But whatever you do,

LOVE

We all have a journey to make. It's called *life*.

THE PRESENT AND FUTURE

I try to walk four or five times a week to keep my blood circulating and get my natural Vitamin D. I continue to take all my natural herbs and vitamins. I pray every morning and night for Gods guidance and strength. I know with the success of Dragon's Breath Salsa and this book, I can keep touching lives and keep giving love and encouragement and hope everywhere I go.

I am still looking for Mr. Right. Someone who accepts me for me, someone who shares my passions, and someone who will love me and let me love him unconditionally. I will know immediately when we meet for I have dreams of him. There are worse things than being alone, but OMG, it is so good being in love with someone who loves you.

FUTURE LOVE?

The dream appears night after night.
A smile, a touch,
An embrace I want so much.
The need grows stronger in both of us you cannot miss.
The hunger turns to fire with just a kiss.
In my dream I see your eyes staring back at me.
Who is this mystery man, God? Is he my destiny?

God answered saying, "I'll send you an angel, someone you need and who will need you. For it is time to love again. You need laughter and passion in your life again for however long it will last. Whatever your spirit needs, I will send. What you choose to do is up to you. To love is my greatest gift, a gift to give away to others. Go, love and give my gift away."

PSALM 118:17

I shall not die, but live,
And declare the works of the Lord.

This is not THE END, for my life is still unfolding.

INFORMATION

If you would like to have information about my Herbalist, please e-mail me at,

barbara.mann1017@gmail.com

IT'S JUST ME RECIPES

There is no rhyme or reason for the recipes I wrote other than the love I have for each person associated with the recipes. I did not start out to write some crazy cook book. I just wanted to tell a story, a story that led to hope and inspiration. Since I am such a foodie, the recipes just seem to fall in place with the story. Some of the recipes are my original and some are adapted from someone else's recipe. But, I shared them with you through deep love. Love for people, our existence, our compassion for one another, our understanding of our differences and how that makes who and what we are. I think food has replaced music as the universal language because we can share and taste different cultures. What better way to experience life than one spoonful at a time. Of course, add some music and you have a party!

I have never had any formal culinary training. I'm not a gourmet cook. All I know is if I think of a dish, I want to cook it and eat it and have others enjoy it as well as they are my best critics, but I am my own worst critic. I may change the recipe a little each time I prepare it trying to enhance the experience. I consider myself a dump and pour cook, so when I started thinking about the recipes, I knew I had to cook each one, taking time to measure each ingredient. This was challenging for me as I would get half way through the recipe and realize I didn't measure and write down one or even two of the ingredients having to start all over again. So I hope you find something in the recipe section that sparks your taste buds enough to try. I also hope the recipes are not too complicated. I tried to keep them simple, but sometimes simple just doesn't have the depth and taste. You can try one or two and see what you think, change them if you like. Make them your own.

You may notice that many of the recipes are seafood. I absolutely love seafood and have many happy memories related to eating the fresh east coast offerings. You may also notice that I have not "lightened" the recipes. They are what they are, just dishes I love.

RECIPES

Growing up on Virginia's Chesapeake Bay, we usually had a variety of fresh seafood. Dad would catch fresh fish, blue crabs and rake for oysters and clams. Mom would make oyster stew, clam chowder, fry fresh fish crispy in corn meal and steam the crabs. I loved the taste of the oyster stew but would not eat the oysters and I loved the crab cakes and things Mom made with the crab meat, but I just couldn't pick out the crab meat from the shells. There was too much "mess" under the shells.

One weekend visiting Renee and Jim's parents in Mann's Harbor, Pop suggested we have some steamed crabs. I said I didn't like them and told him why. Pop laughed and said, "Ole girlie, I'll cook you some crabs you will like". Pop and Jim left and came back with a bushel of crabs and proceeded to "clean" them on the back of his pickup truck. Using gloves, they took a live crab and tore off the top shell, scraped off the lungs, cut off the eyes and pulled off the back flap. Then Pop handed it to me to spray with the water hose. To my amazement, I held a clean, beautiful crab, ready to steam. Pop layered the clean crabs in an empty lard can adding salt and pepper. Then he mixed vinegar and red pepper flakes and poured over the crabs. Put on the lid and steamed. They were the best. No heavy seasonings covered the crab flavor. I sat on a blanket under a large tree all afternoon picking and eating the crab meat. After that day, I always clean my crabs before steaming. Pop and Mary cooked other wonderful dishes. One of my OTHER favorite dishes is baked fresh caught striped bass rock fish with sliced potatoes, onions, and bacon. It was simple but delicious. And Pop always made hush puppies.

I thought it fitting to give you a recipe for Crab Soup and Hush Puppies.

CRAB SOUP

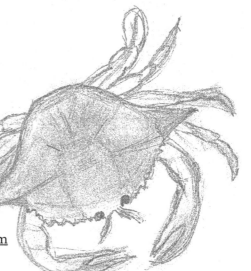

6 Tablespoons butter – 2 for sauté and 4 for roux
4 Tablespoons finely chopped celery
4 Tablespoons finely chopped bell pepper
2 Scallions, thinly sliced, some green
2 Tablespoons chopped parsley (fresh is best)
1 ½ cups fresh white mushrooms, chopped small
4 Tablespoons flour
½ Teaspoon nutmeg, fresh grated if possible
1 Teaspoon hot sauce like Tabasco or Franks
2 Tablespoon Worcestershire sauce
2 Tablespoons Old Bay Seafood Seasoning, low sodium
½ Teaspoon salt
1 Teaspoon black pepper

---

4 Cups heavy cream

3 Cups ½ and ½

½ Cup or less good cooking Sherry

1 ½ Pounds lump crab, any cartilage removed. Fresh is best. May use fresh Dungeness. King or Snow crab meat is ok but it can be salty. Do NOT use imitation crab.

Melt 2 tablespoons butter in large pot over medium heat. Add onions, celery, green pepper and mushrooms, sauté until just tender, about 5 to 7 minutes. Add 4 tablespoons butter and flour. Cook for about 4 minutes making light golden roux. Wisk in heavy cream over medium heat stirring until it is thick and smooth. Wisk in ½ and ½, black pepper, Tabasco, Worcestershire, and Old Bay (if you are not a fan of Old Bay, start by adding 1 tablespoon and taste before adding second tablespoon), nutmeg, parsley. Stir and simmer until smooth and creamy, but do not boil. Add crab and lightly stir until hot, again, do not boil. Remove from heat. Sherry can be added just before serving. Here again you should add half and taste and then add the other half if you wish or let each person add their own. Serve with Hush Puppies.

HUSH PUPPIES

1 Cup Quaker yellow corn meal

½ Cup all-purpose flour

1 Teaspoon onion powder

1 Teaspoon salt

1 Tablespoon sugar

1 Teaspoon baking soda

2 Tablespoon melted butter

¾ Cup buttermilk

1 Egg, beaten

Peanut oil or vegetable oil for deep frying

In large bowl, mix corn meal, flour, onion powder, salt, sugar, baking soda. In small bowl, mix butter, buttermilk and egg. Stir into dry ingredients, mixing well. Let rest until oil is heated. Heat about 4 to 5 inches of oil in a pot or deep fryer to 350 degrees. Drop tablespoon size of batter into hot oil. Deep fry until golden brown, around 5 minutes. I always cut open the first one to make sure it is cooked all the way through and adjust time if needed. Fry in small batches and drain on paper towels.

CRY BABY PUPPIES

Use Hush Puppies recipe and add 3 small Habanero peppers, finely chopped with seeds in processor, to batter. Follow Hush Puppies cooking instructions. These are hot and wonderful.

OTHER VARIATIONS FOR HUSH PUPPIES:

¼ Cup finely chopped onion – or
¼ Cup chopped fresh chives – or
¼ Cup sharp cheddar cheese – and/or
1 Jalapeno, seeded and finely chopped

If you love blue crabs, you have to try fried soft shell blue crabs. I, of course, shied away from them at first because they were cooked with the top shell on and when I bit into the crab, it squished out juices and the yellow/green "mess" I didn't like in steamed crabs. So I decided that the deliciousness (is that even a word?) was too good to pass up and decided to clean my soft blue crabs the same way I did my hard crabs, removing the top shell and cleaning out the lungs and any "mess". I tried them fried in a pancake-like batter but thought it was too heavy. I fry them in a simple beer batter so not to take away from their special rich flavor.

BEER BATTERED SOFT BLUE CRABS

12 Soft blue crabs, <u>cleaned</u>, <u>patted</u> <u>dry</u>
¾ Cup corn starch
¼ Cup rice or plain flour
1 Teaspoon baking powder
1 Teaspoon Old Bay Seafood seasoning, I use low sodium
¼ Teaspoon pepper
1 Egg slightly beaten
½ Cup <u>cold</u> beer
Peanut oil for frying

Heat peanut oil in deep fryer or pot to 375 degrees.

In large bowl, mix corn starch, flour, baking powder, Old Bay, pepper. Add ¼ cup of beer and egg and mix. Add beer as needed a little at a time until your batter is smooth and thin but not too thin. You want it to cover your crabs well.

Dip each crab in batter and drop in oil, two or three at a time depending on how large your fryer is, no more. You don't want to over crowd. Fry turning, until golden brown. Do not overcook.

Crabs are like shrimp, they can overcook easily. Remove with slotted spoon and drain single layer on paper towels.

For anyone who has never eaten a soft crab, you eat the whole thing, legs and shell and all. A soft crab is one that has just shed its outer hard shell, called peeler crabs, so it can grow bigger. They need to be harvested very quickly after shedding as the new shell will start hardening and it will no longer be a soft crab. Duh. I think I said all of that right.

BEER BATTERED HARD CRABS

Use this batter and deep fry some hard crabs. Make sure they are <u>cleaned</u> the way I described Pop and Jim cleaned and prepared them for steaming. These are delicious. Whoa! I'm starting a crab craving. Super Bowl is coming up and I wish I had a bushel of steamed crabs, sit in front of the TV, watch the game and pick crabs. Yum. If you batter them, you can have your beer and eat it too.

You can use this recipe for shrimp and fish. If you omit the Old Bay and add ½ teaspoon of salt, you can fry vegetables, chicken and stuffed peppers (Jalapenos) with cream cheese and bacon or cream cheese and chopped shrimp or crab.

Did you ever taste something and in that moment you knew you would love it for life? That is how I felt the first time I tasted real fresh caught shrimp. There is nothing like that taste. Each year during shrimp season, we would go to the fish docks in Wanchese, North Carolina and get fresh caught shrimp off the shrimp boats. We purchased fifty to a hundred pounds, pop the heads off, wash and freeze in water in one to two pound containers. We had fresh shrimp all year long. I love shrimp and it can be cooked so many wonderful ways.

A couple years ago while visiting Renee, Darren, Ashley and Adrian, I mentioned Shrimp and Grits. I'm a southern girl and have eaten grits all my life, so Darren went to the local fish house in Hatteras and got fresh shrimp and Renee cooked shrimp and grits for dinner. Yummy. It was really great with fresh shrimp and cheesy grits. So here is my Shrimp and Grits recipe with a little flavor twist. Layers of flavor.

SHRIMP AND GRITS

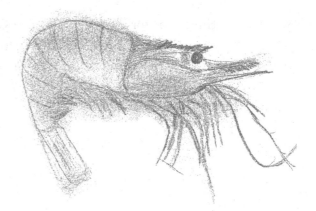

¼ Cup butter
½ Cup diced onion
½ Cup finely chopped celery
½ Cup finely chopped green bell pepper
½ Cup finely chopped red bell pepper
2 Cloves garlic, pressed
1 15 oz. can tomato sauce
8 oz. chicken broth
1 Teaspoon Parsley flakes
¼ Teaspoon dried Thyme
¼ Teaspoon dried Oregano leaves
2 Bay leaves
2 Teaspoons McCormick Cajun seasoning
1 Teaspoon Worcestershire sauce
1 pound raw peeled, deveined shrimp, 31-40 count is a good size.
Strained liquid from 1 pint fresh oysters-save oysters to fry later or add them if you like. Very rich flavor.

Melt butter in large, deep skillet. Add onion, celery, peppers, and garlic and sauté 5 minutes over medium heat. Add tomato sauce, broth, parsley, thyme, oregano, bay leaves, Cajun seasoning and Worcestershire sauce. Cover and simmer 10 minutes, medium heat.

Add shrimp and oyster liquid, bring back to simmer and simmer uncovered for 10 to 15 minutes or until shrimp are cooked. Remove Bay leaves. Serve over grits.

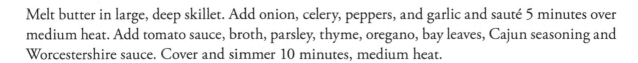

GRITS

4 Cups water
1 Cup Quaker quick 5 minute grits
1 Teaspoon salt
3 Tablespoon butter
1 Cup shredded Sharp Cheddar Cheese
1 Cup shredded Colby Jack Cheese

Bring water and salt to a boil in medium pot. Add grits and stir until they boil and bubble, reduce heat to low and cover. Cook 5 to 7 minutes, stirring until thick. Remove from heat and stir in butter and cheeses until blended and creamy. Serve with shrimp on top.

Personal note: I don't eat oysters, but I love the flavor. Mom would make oyster stew and many, well ok, all of us children would just eat the milk of the stew so Mom and Dad ate all the oysters. When Mom made oyster stuffing one year at Thanksgiving, I tried it because what's Thanksgiving without stuffing. I found a little, tiny, baby crab in my stuffing. Dad teased and said I had to eat it. I cried. I didn't want to eat it or any of the stuffing, so after that Mom made both plain and oyster stuffing. When I had my business and traveled to New Orleans many times, I loved to eat gumbo. It was dark and rich. And then I found an oyster in it and everyone laughed at me, so each time I ordered the gumbo, I picked out the oysters and gave them to my friends. I don't know why, I love the flavor but cannot eat the oyster. And when I am at Renee's, Darren, God bless him, makes my Clams Casino with just the clam strips. There is just something about the green goo mess. And no, no mussels either.

Lloyd loved to hunt and fish. We usually had fish and venison in the freezer so I wasn't surprised when he walked in one day with a recipe he tore out of a magazine. I had never heard of this dish before so I was as excited as he was to try it. We used ground venison sausage we made instead of pork sausage and rock fish, but I have made it with pork sausage and Cod fish. This dish is hearty and is great on a cold, rainy winter's day watching football in front of a warm fire.

FISH MUDDLE

1 Pound HOT ground pork sausage/ Jimmy_Dean
2 Pounds skinless, boneless fish fillets, cut in large cube size pieces. Use Cod, Grouper, Rock or any firm chowder fish.
½ Cup bread crumbs mixed with 4 to 5 tablespoons water
½ Cup minced green onions for meatballs
½ Cup sliced green onions
½ Cup finely chopped celery
1 Egg, beaten
1 Teaspoon Oregano
¼ Teaspoon Thyme
¼ Teaspoon sage
½ Teaspoon pepper and ½ teaspoon salt for meatballs
¼ Teaspoon Allspice
1 Cup chicken broth, low sodium
6 cups ½ and ½
1 ½ Teaspoons salt and ½ teaspoon pepper for ½ and ½
¼ Cup instant mashed potatoes
1 Tablespoon chopped parsley
2 Tablespoons butter

Mix bread crumbs, ½ cup minced onions, egg, oregano, thyme, sage, salt and pepper. Add sausage and mix thoroughly. For each meatball, use 1 tablespoon mixture. Spray bottom of large pot with cooking spray, add meatballs and brown, add other ½ cup of onions and celery, and cook for just a minute or two. Add broth, bring to boil, reduce heat, cover and simmer until meatballs are done, about 10 minutes. Place fish on top of meatballs. Add salt, pepper and allspice to ½ and ½, mix and pour over fish. Simmer until the fish flakes with a fork. Stir in instant potatoes, parsley, butter and heat until mixture thickens. Remove from heat and let it rest for flavors to come together. Serve with crusty bread.

This is also a recipe from Lloyd. It is for refrigerator pickles. They are easy to make and are really good with barbequed meats. I like them on a cracker with a piece of cheese.

REFRIGERATOR PICKLES

6 Cups thinly sliced English cucumbers, do not peel
2 Medium onions thinly sliced
1 ¾ Cups sugar
1 Cup white vinegar
2 Tablespoons salt
1 Teaspoon celery seed

Layer the cucumbers and onions in a bowl. Mix sugar, vinegar, salt, and celery seed until sugar is dissolved. Pour over cucumbers and onions. Cover and refrigerate for 24 hours. These will keep for up to 6 weeks if they last that long.

My father was a meat and potato man. If there was no meat on his plate, he wanted to know why and when he would have it on his plate. He loved vegetables, but with meat. When I was taking care of Dad, he started having trouble chewing meat like steak so I would cook cuts of meat that were very tender and flavorful. This recipe was one of his favorite. The pork was very tender with, yes you guessed it, potatoes.

PORK CHOP CASSEROLE

1 Package assorted pork chops-these are the cheaper cut, mostly dark meat with bone
6 Russet potatoes, peeled and sliced thin
1 Large onion, peeled and sliced thin
1 10oz. can cream of mushroom soup
1 ½ Cups of shredded Colby or sharp Cheddar cheese
Salt and Pepper, Garlic powder, Paprika and Onion powder

Remove bones from pork chops; remove as much fat as you can. Lightly sprinkle salt, pepper, paprika and garlic and onion powder on both sides of pork chops. Place single layer in baking dish sprayed with cooking spray. Cover with foil. Bake 375 degrees for 15 minutes, turn chops over, cover and bake for another 10 minutes. There should be juices in the baking dish. Pour juices in bowl, add soup and blend. Pour mixture over pork chops. Toss onions and potatoes with small amount of salt and pepper, about ¼ to ½ teaspoon each and layer potatoes and onions over pork chops. Cover with foil. Bake until potatoes are tender and casserole is bubbling. Remove and discard foil and sprinkle with cheese. Bake until cheese is golden brown. Serve with your favorite green vegetable.

Dad also loved cornbread. This recipe was given to me many years ago and I have had to substitute the cornbread mix as I can no longer find the kind listed in the original recipe, but it is still buttery and moist and goes great with chili, pulled barbequed pork, ribs, soups or just about anything. Heck, just grab a piece for a snack.

HEAVENLY CORNBREAD

1 Stick of butter, divided in half
3 Boxes Jiffy cornbread mix
1 Cup sour cream
1 Can Creamed Corn
3 Tablespoons sugar
3 Eggs, beaten

Heat the oven to 350 degrees. Mix cornbread mix, ½ stick of melted butter, sour cream, can corn, sugar and eggs until blended. In oven, melt ½ stick of butter in 9 x 13 baking pan. Remove from oven and pour cornbread mix over hot butter in baking pan. Bake until done in center and golden brown. Test center with toothpick. It usually takes about 50 minutes.

You can add jalapeno peppers and/or sharp cheddar cheese to spice things up.

Mom was such a wonderful cook. Feeding seven children was no easy task. I would stay in the kitchen and watch her mix up cakes and pies; make the best biscuits and fried chicken. How unfortunate it was that Mom did not write down many of her recipes. A few of us children have one or two of our favorite recipes, but not many. After her death, I realized that those wonderful smells and tastes would only live on in my memories. I have tried to duplicate, but the recipes never turned out the same. I have two pie recipes that I love. The Sweet Potato Pie is really simple, but delicious. I like it better than pumpkin. But I am a choc-a-holic, so this is my favorite. If you like chocolate, really like chocolate, this one is for you.

CHOCOLATE PIE

½ Cup plus 2 teaspoon Cocoa powder
2 Tablespoons butter
½ Cup flour-either kind
1 Cup sugar
¼ Teaspoon salt
2 ½ Cups scalded milk
3 Eggs, separated
1 Teaspoon Vanilla extract
6 Tablespoons sugar for egg whites
Cream of Tartar-1/8 teaspoon per egg white
1 Deep dish pie shell, 9", baked and cooled

In a double boiler, melt butter. Mix cocoa, flour, sugar, and salt and add to butter. Add scalded milk and stir constantly until mixture is good and thick. While mixture is thickening, beat egg yolks and temper with some of chocolate mixture. Stir tempered egg yolks into chocolate mixture in pot and cook until <u>thick</u>. This mixture will be lumpy but keep stirring and it will smooth out. Remove from heat, stir in vanilla and let cool a little. Pour into pie shell.

Egg whites should be room temperature. Beat egg whites and cream of tartar on high until peaks form. Continue beating, gradually adding sugar a little at a time and continue to beat until all the sugar is dissolved and you have stiff peaks. Spread over top of pie bringing meringue to edge to seal. Bake in preheated oven 425 degrees for 4 to 5 minutes to lightly brown. Remove and cool completely.

Personal note: I am not a fan of meringue so I usually chill my pie and use whipped topping.

SWEET POTATO PIE

5 Large eggs
3 1/2 Cups mashed sweet potatoes/4 large sweet potatoes
2 Cups sugar
1 Stick of Butter, melted
12 oz. Can evaporated milk
3 Teaspoon Vanilla extract
1 Teaspoon Cinnamon
2 Pie shells, 9"

Wash sweet potatoes, dry and rub with a little vegetable oil. Place in a pan and bake in 350 degrees oven for about an hour or until soft and done. Try not to puncture skin during baking. Once done, cool and remove potato from skin, mash and measure 3 1/2 packed cups and set aside. Don't worry about strings, some will break up while mixing and some will stick to beaters. Just remove beaters and rinse off and continue to beat. I personally like the texture. With electric mixer, beat eggs until foamy. Add sugar and beat until light, add sweet potatoes. Beat well. Add melted butter, milk and vanilla and cinnamon. Beat until well blended. Fill FROZEN pie shells. Bake 50 to 55 minutes at 375 degrees. Pie is done when knife comes out clean. Cool and serve with whipped topping.

Note: When baking pies, if the crust starts to brown too quickly, put a thin piece of foil around the crust and continue to bake until filling is done. Nothing worse than a pie with a burnt crust.

In Virginia, Sherrill, my hair dresser for 20 years who recently died of lung cancer, grew vegetables every year in her garden. One of our favorite was yellow crook neck squash. She always gave me some to take home. One day she said she had been making casseroles but they were watery. I gave her a recipe I adapted from a cook book Renee gave me. I changed a few things and added cheese making this a really creamy and flavorful casserole. After a while, I asked Sherrill about the squash casserole. She said it was the best and she had been making and freezing them. All her friends and family loved it, too. I laughed and said that must be why she hadn't given me fresh squash lately. We both laughed and she sent me home with a bag of fresh squash that day.

YELLOW SQUASH CASSEROLE

6 Large or 12 small yellow squash, sliced
1 Large onion, thinly sliced
1 4oz. jar diced pimientos, with juice, do not drain
2 Cups sharp cheddar cheese
1 Stick of butter
1 Box Stove Top Cornbread Stuffing Mix
1 10oz. can Cream of Chicken Soup
1 Cup sour cream
Salt and Pepper

In a large pot of water, add 1 teaspoon salt. Add sliced onions and squash. Bring to a boil and cook until the squash is just fork tender. Do not overcook. Drain as much water as possible. In a large casserole dish, melt butter in oven. Remove from oven and stir dry stuffing mix into the butter. Remove one cup of stuffing mix for topping. Spread the rest over bottom of casserole dish. In large bowl mix cream of chicken soup, sour cream, cheese and pimientos. Stir in squash and onion and ½ teaspoon black pepper. Spoon the squash mixture over stuffing in casserole dish. Sprinkle reserved stuffing mix over top. Bake in 350 oven until bubbly and brown, about 40 to 50 minutes. Cool at least 15 minutes before serving.

After Jim died, my girlfriends, sister and I would go to a musical and out to dinner once a month. One of our favorite places was a small restaurant near the ocean. I always ordered a fresh tuna dish when offered as the chef's special. Everything except the pasta was cooked at our table. Garlic, olive oil, seared tuna, marinara and then the noodles were added. All of this was put in the middle of a huge wheel of Parmesan cheese. The chef would scrape the melting cheese and blend it with the hot tuna and pasta and serve. What a wonderful dish. I have tried to duplicate the dish, but the cheese wheel was the secret. I came close. When I couldn't get fresh tuna, I substituted fresh jumbo shrimp. Sometimes I would add a few sliced mushrooms, some green onion and a handful of fresh spinach to the shrimp.

TUNA PASTA MARINARA

1 Pound fresh Ahi Tuna, cut into bite size pieces, sprinkled with salt and pepper
1 16oz. container good marinara or you can make your own, it's really easy
8 oz. of pasta, Fettuccini, Linguini, or Spaghetti, just about any you like
2 Cloves garlic, minced
2 Tablespoons extra-virgin olive oil
1 Tablespoon butter
8 oz. Parmesan cheese
1 Tablespoon salt
Chopped fresh Basil at least ¼ cup, more if you like it as I do, remember it is a healing herb

In large pot, bring water and tablespoon of salt to a boil. Add noodles and cook according to directions. While noodles are cooking, in a large skillet, add olive oil and butter and heat to medium high adding garlic. Sizzle garlic for about 30 seconds, do not burn. Add tuna pieces and sear quickly, a few at a time. Remove and add next few. Too many pieces at one time will not sear, but steam. Tuna should not be cooked all the way, should be pink inside if possible. This will help keep it from getting too dry and retain flavor. Return all pieces of tuna to pan and add marinara and heat to simmer. Drain pasta well, add hot tuna marinara to hot noodles, and stir in cheese until melted and creamy. Serve and garnish with chopped fresh basil.

When P was staying with me, one night I made this recipe using the shrimp, mushrooms, onion and baby spinach. He liked it so much, he cooked it for friends and family. I always laughed when he called me from the grocery store and asked for the ingredients. Using recipe above-

1 Pound fresh large shrimp, shelled, deveined and drained/substitute for tuna
Add:
½ Cup fresh sliced mushrooms
2 Green scallions, thinly sliced, some green
1 Large handful of fresh baby spinach leaves/I like to pinch off the little bit of stem

In large pot, bring water and salt to a boil. Add noodles and cook according to directions. While cooking noodles, in a large skillet, heat olive oil and butter, heat to medium high and add garlic, sizzle for 30 seconds, add shrimp and sear on both sides, a few at a time. Same as with tuna, too many will not sear, but steam. After removing seared shrimp, add mushrooms and onion and sauté quickly until tender but not overcooked. Return shrimp and add marinara sauce. Heat to a simmer and add spinach, cook until it is just wilted. Drain pasta well and add hot shrimp marinara and cheese to hot pasta. Stir until cheese is melted and creamy. Serve and garnish with fresh Basil.

While running my business in Virginia Beach, I met many really nice people, becoming friends with a business owner nearby. She happen to mention that she and her daughter were going to get 10 cent scallops in bacon and would I like to come. Well, hell yes! Scallops are so sweet and yummy wrapped in bacon. Little did I know, they were deep fried until the bacon was crispy. I ate until I was ready to pop. It's the only way I like bacon wrapped scallops now. I hate undercooked bacon and if you broil or bake until the bacon is done, the scallops are dry. Deep frying leaves them moist in the middle and the bacon is crispy and believe it or not, they are less greasy cooked this way. You can serve these on a bed of dressed baby mixed greens, or with couscous with fresh pesto (my favorite), or on a toothpick and just eat them!

BACON WRAPPED SCALLOPS

2 Pounds large or medium scallops, washed, foot removed, and patted dry
1 Pound hickory smoked bacon but not sugar cured, cut in pieces that will wrap around Scallop overlapping just enough to secure with toothpick. Do not double wrap.
Toothpicks
Vegetable oil for deep frying

In large pot or deep fryer with fry basket, heat 5 to 6 inches of oil to 375 degrees. Wrap each scallop in bacon piece and secure with toothpick. Drop in oil and cook until bacon is crispy. Do not over crowd, a few at a time. Drain well.

Bacon is back, baby, enjoy! Although for me it was never really gone. Love it, love it.

Just before leaving Virginia, W and I became friends and went out to lunch and dinner. We both love calamari and tried it at any restaurant that offered it, looking for the best. This continued on our trips to the Keys, the Gulf coast of Florida, San Francisco and the wine country. We even sampled some in the area where W lives. We both had to agree that a small restaurant on the waterfront in Norfolk, Virginia had the best. Small thin circles lightly breaded and deep fried perfectly with thin sliced breaded Jalapeno peppers. What a great combination. So I bet you think I am going to give you a recipe for fried calamari. Sorry. I have tried to cook it but I always end up with rubber bands. If I were texting, this is where I would text LOL, because my attempts have been laughable. I'll keep trying because I love it so much. So I will tell you about salmon, yum. One time visiting W, I didn't want to go out to dinner in the rainy cold so I decided to cook salmon. We both love it and what's not to love about this delicate fish. I cooked it and served it on a thin toasted piece of bread drizzled with an infused olive oil I made and topped it with chopped tomatoes, peppers, green onion, black olives and feta cheese. Served it with baby mixed greens and pecan brown rice and some really good wine. Who cared if it was raining outside?

SALMON BRUSCHETTA

2 Four or six oz. portions wild caught salmon, boneless and skinless
2 Thin slices Italian bread

Infused olive oil, make your own. To 8 oz. of good extra virgin olive oil add 2 cloves fresh garlic thinly sliced, 1 teaspoon each Basil, Thyme, Rosemary, Oregano, black pepper, 1 teaspoon Worcestershire sauce, 1 teaspoon liquid smoke. Let it marinate for a couple of days, the longer the better, shake a few times. Use on just about anything.

1 Tablespoon butter
4 Tablespoons chopped cherry tomatoes
4 Tablespoons chopped bell pepper
2 Tablespoons scallions, thinly sliced
4 Large pitted black olives sliced thin
4 Tablespoons crumbled Feta cheese
Baby Mixed greens
Salt and Pepper
Balsamic Vinegar

In a skillet that can go into oven, melt butter and add 1 tablespoon infused oil, heat to medium heat, should sizzle when salmon is added. Season the salmon with salt and pepper, to taste. Place salmon top down in pan and cook until a crust forms and salmon is cooked almost half way. Turn salmon over and repeat cooking on other side. Remove pan from heat. Turn on broiler of oven. In bowl, mix tomatoes, pepper, scallions, and olives with 2 tablespoons infused olive oil. Divide and place on top of salmon pieces. Top each salmon piece with 2 tablespoons Feta cheese.

Broil until cheese melts and starts to brown. Remove pan from broiler, let rest. Toast bread just to light brown under broiler. Do not let it get too brown and hard. Brush with infused olive oil.

Placed one slice of bread on each plate and add salmon to the top of bread. Scoop out any tomato mix that fell off and place on salmon. Drizzle with Balsamic vinegar. Add baby green mix, dressed or not to plate. Eat as a salad or add rice for a full meal.

I grow fresh herbs, especially basil. I love fresh made basil Pesto. It tastes so good on noodles, couscous, and pizza, anything you like. I like it on pita with left over salmon. Just take pita rounds and cut them into triangles, place them on a baking sheet, top with a piece of salmon and top with a teaspoon or so of pesto. Place in oven, 350 degrees, until pita starts to get crisp and salmon and pesto are hot. I like to think of this as a healthy snack.

BASIL PESTO

3 Cups fresh basil leaves, packed
½ Cup freshly grated Parmesan cheese
¾ Cup extra virgin olive oil
½ Cup pine nuts toasted lightly and cooled-I don't use walnuts as they can be bitter
3 Garlic cloves, peeled and rough chopped
Salt and pepper to taste

In a food processor, pulse the pine nuts a few times, add garlic and pulse a few times. Add basil and pulse to combine with nuts and garlic. With food processor running, slowly add olive oil and process until everything is starting to get smooth. Stop processor and scrape down sides and add the cheese. Process until well blended. Add salt and pepper to taste. Place in a container in the refrigerator for a day for flavors to come together.

COMPOUND HERB BUTTER

1 Stick of butter, room temperature soft
2 Tablespoon fresh Rosemary leaves removed from stems, finely chopped
1 Tablespoon fresh Thyme leaves removed from stems
2 Tablespoon fresh Basil leaves removed from stems, finely chopped
1 Teaspoon fresh lemon juice

If your butter is really soft as it should be and you have finely chopped your herbs, you should be able to just put everything in a bowl and blend, place on clear wrap, roll up and form a log. Twist ends of clear wrap and place roll in refrigerator until hard again. Slice off what you need. I use it on vegetables like Asparagus, Brussel Sprouts, baked or mashed potatoes, or fish and meats. A pork chop is great cooked with it.

QUICK ASPARAGUS WITH HERB BUTTER

1 Pound fresh Asparagus, tough part of stem removed, washed and drained well, pat dry
1 Tablespoon compound herb butter
Pinch salt and pepper
½ Cup Parmesan cheese, or another kind you like

Turn oven to broil. On a cookie sheet sprayed with cooking spray, arrange asparagus in a single layer. Sprinkle with salt and pepper. Melt butter and drizzle over asparagus. Broil for just 2 to 3 minutes. Turn over and sprinkle cheese over top and broil until the cheese starts to turn brown.

CAPRESE WITH PESTO

Fresh Basil Pesto
2 Medium green or almost green tomatoes trim top and bottom, slice each into 4 slices
1 8 oz. Fresh Mozzarella Cheese ball, cut into 8 slices
½ Cup all-purpose flour
½ Cup Italian seasoned bread crumbs
¼ Cup Panko bread crumbs
2 Egg whites, beaten with 1 tablespoon water
1 Teaspoon each salt and pepper
Oil for frying
Balsamic Vinegar

In first bowl, add flour and season with salt and pepper. Add egg whites and water to second bowl and beat with fork. Mix Italian and Panko bread crumbs in third bowl.

Dust tomato slices with flour, dip in egg whites and then in bread crumbs. Fry in hot oil until brown and crispy. Drain on paper towels and place on cookie sheet. Top with a slice of cheese and a teaspoon Pesto (more if you like). Broil for about 2 to 3 minutes. Cheese will just start to melt. Remove to serving plate with mixed greens and drizzle with Balsamic Vinegar.

LIGHTER CAPRESE WITH PESTO

1 8 oz. Package of rolled Prosciutto and Mozzarella
16 Cherry or Grape tomatoes cut in half lengthways making 32 halves
Fresh Basil Pesto
Fresh Basil leaves for garnish
Balsamic Vinegar
32 toothpicks

Slice Prosciutto and Mozzarella roll into 8 slices and cut each slice in half and each half in half making 32 pieces. Take 1 piece of meat and cheese roll, top with tomato half, flat side up and stick toothpick through them and stand up with roll on bottom. Repeat until you do all 32. Place a small amount of pesto on top of each tomato half. Drizzle with Balsamic vinegar. Garnish with Basil leaves.

While living with my brother Charlie and his family in Florida, I became familiar with the Hispanic culture and food. In Virginia, Taco Bell and Tijuana Flats was the extent of my Hispanic cuisine. Over the years, I have learned to enjoy the different flavors of this cuisine. Slow roasted pork, much like southern pulled pork but with different spices, wonderfully flavored rice, mole sauce rich in flavor, Tamales, simple street tacos and fish and shrimp tacos; fresh Pico De Gallo flavors of cilantro, lime, Jalapeno peppers and other wonderful peppers like Poblano, Serrano and the hot Habanero; fresh seafood Ceviche and Carne Asada are just a few. Surprisingly, most dishes were not as spicy as I had thought. I like hot, so in many of the dishes I made I added some hot spicy peppers. One dish that the whole family liked was enchiladas. There are all kinds of enchiladas, chicken, cheese, steak, and ground beef, pulled pork. You can add refried beans and/or Spanish rice and serve with red sauce, green sauce, or cheese sauce. I kept it simple and did not add any hot as Charlie and Valorie could not tolerate the hot spices.

ENCHILADAS

3 Boneless, skinless chicken breast
1 Large can 28 oz. Las Palmas red enchilada sauce or your own favorite like El Paso
1 Bunch Green onions, chopped
2 Tablespoons Butter
2 Tablespoons Flour
2 Cups ½ and ½
Flour Tortillas, 8 inch or taco size
2 Cups Colby or Sharp Cheddar cheese, shredded
½ Cup fresh cilantro leaves, chopped
Black olives for garnish, optional
Salt and Pepper

In a large pan with lid, place chicken breast with 2 cups of water, season with ½ teaspoon each salt and pepper. Bring to simmer over medium low heat, cover and cook until chicken is tender and done, 165 degrees. Remove to plate and cool. Using two forks, shred chicken into small pieces. Reserve any broth in a bowl. Return chicken to pan, add green onions (reserving 2 tablespoons for garnish), and add 1 cup of enchilada sauce and ½ cup reserved broth. Simmer on low heat for about 5 minutes or until chicken is well seasoned with sauce. Remove from heat, stir in cilantro and let cool. You want this moist and flavorful but not too wet.

In large pot, melt butter over medium heat, stir in flour and cook for 2 to 3 minutes stirring, but do not brown. Add ½ and ½, stirring until it thickens. Add 2 cups of enchilada sauce and stir until mixed. Add 1 cup of cheese. Stir until blended and smooth. Remove from heat.

Fill each tortilla with chicken mixture and roll. Place in baking pan or dish sprayed with cooking spray, seam side down. Bake in oven heated to 375 degrees for 20 minutes until tortillas begin to get crisp and brown on edges. Remove pan and pour sauce over top, as little or as much as you like, sprinkle with 1 cup of cheese, green onions, and some sliced black olives. Bake until cheese has browned, dish is bubbly. Serve with beans and rice.

There may be extra sauce to use on beans and rice or freeze for a later use.

Variations: Use green chili sauce instead of red sauce
Add ½ cup cheese to chicken mix
You can add rice and/or refried beans to tortilla with chicken for a stuffed enchilada
Use pulled pork or beef instead of chicken and add rice to tortilla
Add bell pepper for some crunch
Spice up your sauces by adding one chopped Habanero pepper

Be creative!

Serve with Pico De Gallo

PICO DE GALLO

2 Large Jalapeno peppers, stemmed, seeded, finely chopped
2 Tablespoon green pepper, finely chopped
2 Green onions, sliced thin
12 cherry or grape tomatoes, chopped
One bunch cilantro leaves, chopped
Juice of two limes
Pinch of salt and pepper

Mix all ingredients and refrigerate for at least an hour. Serve on enchiladas, fish or shrimp or regular tacos or rice. Add chopped avocados for more yummy goodness.

Charlie's daughter, my niece Rachael loves Alfredo so I taught her to make it when I left Florida. It is easy and flavorful and once you get the basic recipe, you can add sautéed mushrooms, crisp bacon, prosciutto, cooked chicken or shrimp or yummy crab. Let your taste buds be your guide.

EASY CREAMY ALFREDO

2 Sticks butter, softened
2 Cups heavy cream
2 Cloves garlic, minced with garlic press
2 Cups grated Parmesan cheese
½ Cup grated Asiago cheese
1 8oz. to 12oz. Box of pasta
Fresh chopped basil leaves or 2 to 3 tablespoons fresh basil pesto
Black pepper and salt
Pinch fresh grated Nutmeg

In a large sauce pan, melt 1 Tablespoon butter, add garlic and cook 2 to 3 minutes over low heat. Remove from heat and add the rest of butter and cream and nutmeg, stir until mixed, add cheeses and return to low heat and stir until smooth, remove from heat and add salt and pepper to taste. Remember that parmesan is a bit salty.

Cook pasta according to directions on box, drain and add to sauce. Toss pasta until well blended and creamy, adding pesto if you want at this time or sprinkle with fresh basil. Serve immediately.

When you add ingredients like chicken, add it to the sauce just before you add hot pasta and toss so that all ingredients are coated with sauce.

My friend Gloria and I would have dinner together quite often after a movie on Saturday nights or after church on Sundays. We went to many different restaurants trying different foods. One of her favorite dishes was Shrimp Scampi. I always smiled when I saw it on the menu because I knew she would order it and enjoy every bite.

SHRIMP SCAMPI WITH ANGEL HAIR PASTA

25 Large shrimp (21-25) shelled, deveined and patted dry
4 Cloves garlic minced in garlic press
½ Teaspoon each salt, pepper, paprika
2 Tablespoons butter
2 Tablespoons olive oil
½ Cup bottled clam juice
1 Stick of butter
1 Tablespoon fresh lemon juice
1 Tablespoon fresh chopped parsley
½ Cup grated Parmesan cheese
8 oz. Angel Hair pasta cooked following box directions, drained

In a bowl, mix shrimp with garlic, salt, pepper and paprika. Heat 2 tablespoons each butter and oil in oven safe skillet over medium high heat. Add a few shrimp at a time and sear both sides of shrimp, 1 to 2 minutes each side, remove to bowl and continue searing the shrimp a few at a time until all are seared. Reduce heat to medium low. Deglaze pan with clam juice stirring until juice is simmering. Add butter a tablespoon at a time stirring until melted. Add lemon juice and stir shrimp into mixture. Remove from heat and add pasta and toss. Turn oven to broil. Sprinkle with cheese. Broil until cheese melts. Remove and sprinkle with parsley, serve.

I had a very special client I loved in Florida when I took care of the elderly. Ms. J loved to eat and I enjoyed cooking for her and watching her face and smile when she ate something special. She especially loved the blueberry pancakes I made for her most mornings. One morning there was no fresh blueberries and I didn't want to make plain pancakes so I improvised and made something else she liked very much. I made apple pie pancakes.

APPLE PIE PANCAKES

1 Cup Bisquick Baking Mix
½ Cup Milk
1 Egg
1 Single serve cup of applesauce
2 Teaspoons apple pie spice
1 Banana, sliced
Syrup

Mix Bisquick and spice in a bowl. In a 2 cup measuring cup, measure ½ cup milk, add egg and applesauce. Blend well. Add to Bisquick and stir until blended. This will make three small or two medium pancakes. Spray nonstick spray in medium fry pan over medium heat. Measure 1/3 batter if making small or ½ if making medium pancakes, pouring into heated pan. Cook until top has bubbled and holes appear and bottom is golden light brown. Flip and lightly brown. Serve with a little syrup and sliced banana.

Caring for Dad, I learned how important it was for food to be flavorful and easy to eat. Food, especially meat, would be wasted if it was too chewy and hard to digest not to mention the lost nourishment when he would not eat his meals. He really liked meatloaf. My mom would make a large one to feed all 9 of us. I still make meatloaf because I love meatloaf sandwiches the next day with nutty wheat bread and spicy mustard. My southern roots are showing, y'all!

So when I starting cooking for a really sweet elderly couple, I would make a meatloaf and slice it so they could easily reheat it in the microwave. I would make mashed potatoes, creamed spinach, and other vegetables; lasagna and cut it into squares, chicken pot pie, and soups to name a few. Whatever they wanted that would be an easy reheat with a lot of flavor and nourishment is what I would prepare.

I don't know if any of you like and eat meatloaf, most people don't because it can be dry, it's a love it or hate it kind of thing, but here is my recipe. It will make one really large or two small. I usually make the two small and freeze one so when Sis says, "How about meat loaf?" I'm ready. Sis and I love comfort food once in a while. It brings back memories of Mom and our childhood.

MEATLOAF

1 Pound lean ground turkey
1 Pound lean ground beef
1 Pound ground pork-----you can make it with all turkey, but it will be much drier
2 Eggs
¼ Cup ketchup
¼ Cup Tomato sauce
2 Cups bread, white or wheat, cut into small pieces, soaked in ½ cup chicken or beef broth
1 Package McCormick meat loaf seasoning
1 Tablespoon Worcestershire sauce
1 Teaspoon black pepper
1 Single pack of dry Lipton onion soup mix
1 Cup sliced green onions

In a large bowl, beat eggs and mix in all other ingredients except meats until well blended. Add meats and blend everything together using hands. Make sure there are no big chunks of any one meat. Mixture should look uniformly blended. Preheat oven at 350 degrees. At this point you can decide if you will bake one large loaf or separate and freeze a small one.

Spray large baking dish or pan with cooking spray. Form loaf and place in pan, cover with foil. Bake large loaf for 1 ½ hours or until temperature in center of loaf reaches 165 degrees. Time is about 1 hour for small. Just check your loaf temperature as ovens vary in heating. Close to final minutes of cooking, remove dish and drain juices and any grease. Return to oven uncovered to brown top. If you like the ketchup on top, this is the time to smooth on a bit. Put on the ketchup and let it brown a little. Remove and let rest about 10 minutes before slicing.

Try to save a piece for the next day, toast some bread, heat a slice of the meatloaf with a piece of cheese and make a sandwich with spicy mustard. Love it, but, that's just me.

I love southern California. It is so sunny and beautiful. We only have a little rainy weather and a few cold days during the year. We get some rain December through March and our cold weather usually in January, maybe February. It is in the thirties at night and fifties during the day but to me, it seems 40 below. I freeze but even on the coldest day, I can go out in the sun and get warm.

Our normal weather here in southern California is bright and sunny with mostly moderate temperatures between 60 and 80 degrees. My favorite time is having my morning tea on the back patio. The canyon connects to our back yard and I see so many critters like Coyotes, Road Runners, rabbits, many different birds, butterflies, and lizards. The simple beauty of it all at times takes my breath away, especially when I walk up on a rattlesnake sunning itself. Holy #*^$!

We are fortunate to have fresh fruit and vegetables all year long from a local market, Sprouts. I can always go in and find what I'm looking for, fresh, ready to go, and at the right price. California is known for wine, avocados and almonds. We even have a vineyard that makes almond champagne. It's great. There is always fresh organic everything especially kale which I eat two to three times a month, fresh eggplant that can be cooked so many ways, zucchini and squash and fresh green beans. We love fresh fruit like watermelon, my favorite, and all varieties of berries, oranges, apples and pineapples to name a few. I'm making myself hungry. My sister is borderline vegetarian. She doesn't eat much meat so we eat a lot of fresh fruit and vegetables. Me, I like meat like my Dad, although I do cook meatless meals for sis. I probably eat cheese everyday so I use it in many of my dishes. Fresh salad is always on the menu. I like to think our meals are simple and nourishing and I don't always cook heavy like some of the recipes in this book. They are special treats. I get accused of making people fat as it is.

We like stuffed peppers. We can always find fresh green, red, yellow and orange peppers at the local market. I sometimes make them plain and then sometimes I make them spicy. You can stuff them with whatever you like. I have a simple recipe in which I use Fritos corn chips instead of bread crumbs. It gives the peppers a little boost of flavor.

STUFFED BELL PEPPERS

3 Large peppers, 1 red, 1 yellow, 1 orange-cut in half lengthways, stemmed and seeded.
1 Medium onion, chopped
2 Cloves of garlic, finely minced or pressed with garlic press
1 20oz. package lean ground turkey
4 8oz. cans tomato sauce
3 Tablespoons chili powder
1 Teaspoon paprika
1 Teaspoon salt for peppers
1 Teaspoon each salt and pepper
1 ½ Cups cooked brown rice

1 ½ Cups crushed Frito-Lay corn chips
1 ½ Cups shredded sharp cheddar cheese

Bring a pot of water to boil with 1 teaspoon salt. Add pepper halves and cook until a fork will just go in pepper but still firm. Do not overcook; peppers are best when they still have a little crunch. Drain well and place in baking dish sprayed with cooking spray. Set aside while preparing filling. Preheat oven to 375 degrees.

In large skillet, cook ground turkey with garlic, onions, salt* and pepper, chili powder and paprika. Add tomato sauce and simmer on low stirring often for about 5 minutes. Remove from heat and stir in rice and corn chips until blended, spoon into pepper halves, overfilling is ok, and spooning any leftover filling around peppers in pan. Top with cheese. Bake until cheese is golden brown.

For spicy peppers:

Sub one 8 oz. can of tomato sauce with one 10 oz. can of original Ro-Tel diced tomatoes and green chilies.

½ Cup canned corn, drained.

Omit 2 tablespoons chili powder and add 1 package McCormick Hot Taco seasoning mix.

*Do not add teaspoon of salt to mix until you taste for salt flavor. If it is not salty enough with the McCormick seasoning, then add the extra salt.

You can make them as hot as you like.

So for our meatless Mondays, I make eggplant parmesan, or soups like lentil, bean and barley, cream of potato, butternut squash with pear, or white lasagna. The white lasagna has vegetables and a lot of flavor. I use jar Alfredo sauce to keep it simple. Of course, I have been known to cook me an Italian sausage to eat with my lasagna. What?!! I never said I was anywhere near vegetarian.

VEGGIE WHITE LASAGNA

6 Large mushrooms, sliced. About 1 ¼ to 1 ½ cups
1 Small bunch sliced green onions, about ½ cup
1 Small zucchini shredded, about 1 cup
1 Cup spinach, frozen chopped, thawed and squeezed dry or fresh steamed
2 Tablespoons butter
½ Teaspoon each salt and pepper

2 Cups part skim Ricotta cheese
2 Eggs, beaten
½ Teaspoon garlic powder
1 Cup Touch of Philadelphia Italian 5 cheese blend
1 Cup shredded mozzarella cheese
½ Cup Italian 5 cheese for topping
¼ Cup mozzarella for topping
¼ Cup Italian bread crumbs for topping
6 Barilla oven ready lasagna noodles, do not cook
2 Jars Classico Alfredo Sun-dried tomato sauce

Topping- ½ cup 5 cheese blend and ¼ cup mozzarella cheese, mixed with ¼ cup Italian bread crumbs

Preheat oven to 350 degrees

In sauce pan, melt butter and add mushrooms and onions. Sauté for until mushrooms and onions are tender. Add zucchini and spinach, salt and pepper, stirring until mixed, 2 to 3 minutes until hot. Remove from heat.

In large bowl, mix Ricotta cheese, eggs, garlic powder, cheeses until blended and eggs are well incorporated. Add veggie mixture to cheese mixture and blend.

In another bowl, empty both jars of Alfredo sauce.

Spray a baking dish, 9x9, with cooking spray. Spread bottom with ¼ of sauce and place two oven ready lasagna noodles over sauce. Using small spoon, place small amounts of cheese/veggie mix on noodles. Using spoon, press small amounts and smooth mixture covering as much of noodles as possible. You should have used half of mixture. Spoon Alfredo sauce over cheese mixture using about ¼ of mixture and layer next two noodles. Repeat steps using all of cheese mixture and then add another ¼ of sauce. You should have enough sauce left for top. Layer last two noodles on top and spoon last ¼ of sauce on top covering all of noodles. Sprinkle with Topping mixture.

Place on a foil covered cookie sheet and bake for about 1 hour until bubbly and topping is browned. You should check center with thermometer to make sure it is at least 165 degrees or hotter. Remove from oven and let rest 30 minutes before cutting. If top is browning too quickly before center gets hot, cover loosely with foil to prevent top from burning.

I like this and other lasagnas better the next day. I guess all the flavors have had time to blend, kind of like cold pizza.

One Christmas, Kay, KC and Casey Michael came to visit me in Virginia Beach. After Christmas we went to Washington DC to see the museums and monuments. There was snow but it was a real treat for Casey Michael who, living in California, was not used to seeing and playing in it. The morning we left, we stopped off the interstate at Cracker Barrel for breakfast. Since it was Christmas, they still had their trees decorated. We happen to find little Santa and Snowmen ornaments hanging on the trees. They were small with long dangly twiggy looking arms and legs twisted onto the body with small eye hooks. They were so cute and funny, we decided to purchase all we could find for family and friends and of course, for our own trees. So for lunch, we stopped at the next Cracker Barrel and purchased all of the Santa and Snowmen we could find. This was so funny because some were missing arms or legs and we would take the arms or legs off of one and screw them on the others making them complete. So on our return trip as we traveled back to Virginia Beach, sis and I decided to give it one more try and we, yes we did, stopped at Cracker Barrel for dinner. We found a few Snowmen but only one good Santa. When we left, we felt so bad because we left a Santa hanging on the tree with no arms and legs at all. We all actually laughed until we cried, it was so funny. We had enough for family and friends and we decorate our tree every year with our Santa and Snowmen ornaments and remember our trip and laugh about the poor armless and legless Santa we left on the tree. BUT, we never got coal in our stockings! I think Santa has a sense of humor.

While in Washington, we had dinner at our hotel one night after a long day of sightseeing and fun. We were tired and just wanted something simple to eat and go to our rooms and rest up for the next day. Sis and I had salad and decided to split a Crab Quesadilla. It had sweet, succulent Maryland blue crab, fresh spinach, and cheese and right on top in the middle was a scoop of sweet, creamy coleslaw. OMG it was really, really good. I have made this several times and find that you have to have the right coleslaw. I know it sounds silly, but the coleslaw has to be sweet and creamy and not a lot of vinegar. It somehow enhances the crab.

CRAB AND SPINACH QUESADILLA
WITH CREAMY COLESLAW

1 Pint lump crab meat, any cartilage removed, drained
2 Cups Monterey Jack cheese, shredded
½ Cup Garden Vegetable cream cheese
1 Bag fresh baby spinach leaves
8 Medium tortillas
Softened butter
I 14oz. Bag 3 color coleslaw mix
2/3 Cup Kraft Mayonnaise
2 Tablespoons sour cream
3 Tablespoons sugar
2 Teaspoons white wine vinegar

½ Teaspoon salt
½ Teaspoon pepper
Old Bay seasoning

In large bowl mix mayo, sour cream, sugar, vinegar, salt and pepper. Stir in bag of coleslaw. It will look like there is not enough sauce, but just keep stirring until blended. Refrigerate until serving time, at least 2 hours. Stir when ready to use.

Lay out all eight tortillas. Mix Jack cheese and cream cheese and spread on each tortilla to 1 inch of outer edge. Place two layers of spinach leaves on top of cream cheese on 4 of tortillas and then ¼ of crab on top of spinach. Sprinkle a very <u>small</u> amount of Old Bay on crab. Place tortilla on top and press together. The cheese on each tortilla will bind them together. Spread a small amount of butter on the top of tortilla.

Heat large fry pan to medium low heat (if you cook too fast, it will burn before it gets hot inside and cheese melts and spinach wilts), place quesadilla in pan butter side down and brown, spread small amount of butter on top of tortilla in pan and flip over. Brown the other side. Remove to cutting board and let rest about 5 minutes. Cut with pizza cutter in triangles and transfer to serving plate. Place scoop of coleslaw in middle of quesadilla at triangle points. Sooooo Good!

After my cancer surgery, my Herbalist told me to juice fresh kale and drink one to two ounces each day. It is a high antioxidant and I did this for six months cleansing my body. I still love kale and eat it often. It seems that everyone has finally discovered its wonderful flavor as well as its healing properties.

I love stuffed cabbage so I thought why not just eat stuffed kale instead. So I tried it and love its mild flavor stuffed with ground pork and rice, simmered in a spicy tomato sauce. I also make a kale soup and a cauliflower dish with spinach and kale. Eat up, it's good for you.

KALE, SMOKED SAUSAGE, BEAN SOUP

1 Hillshire Farm, 14 oz. package smoked sausage, beef or whichever you like, sliced
1 Bunch of Kale, stems removed, leaves torn into small pieces
1 Can S&W, 15.5 oz., White Chili Beans, with onion, garlic, chili spices, mild Jalapenos, Rinsed and drained
½ Cup chopped onion
½ Cup chopped green bell pepper
1 Carton, 32 oz. chicken broth
½ Teaspoon each salt and pepper
¼ Teaspoon fresh Thyme leaves
1 Teaspoon hot sauce
1 Tablespoon vegetable oil

In a large pot, heat oil and brown the sliced sausage. Add onion and bell pepper and cook a few minutes until tender. Add broth and bring to a boil, reduce heat and add kale, beans, thyme leaves, salt, pepper and hot sauce. Simmer until kale is tender. Serve with my cornbread.

NOT YOUR USUAL POT PIE

2 Small boneless, skinless chicken breast, cooked and chopped into small pieces/2 cups
1 Package of Puff Pastry, 2 sheets, thawed room temperature
1 Head of Cauliflower trimmed and cut into chunks.
1 Teaspoon minced garlic
1 Cup of chopped onion
¼ Cup ½ and ½
¼ Cup chicken broth
4 oz. Philadelphia cream cheese with bacon
1 Bag, 13.25 oz. baby spinach and baby kale mix, pinch off any large stems
1 Cup smoked shredded Cheddar cheese

1 Cup shredded Swiss cheese
1 Egg and 1 tablespoon water for egg wash

Place cauliflower in a pot with garlic, onion, ½ and ½ and chicken broth. Cover and simmer until tender. This will take at least 15 minutes. Mash with a potato masher and stir in cream cheese until smooth, stir in cheeses, stir in chicken, cover and set aside.

Place spinach and kale mix in a glass bowl. Cover and microwave for 2 minutes, stirring halfway through. Press with fork or large spoon while draining juices. Set aside.

Lightly spray a 9 x 9 baking dish with cooking spray. Preheat oven to 375 degrees.

Roll out first pastry sheet on floured surface to 10 x 10. Place in baking dish and bring pastry up the sides to top of dish. Spoon ½ of chicken and cauliflower mix into pastry. Top evenly with all of the spinach and kale mix. Spoon the rest of chicken mix over greens.

Roll out second pastry sheet. Mix egg and water for wash. Bush top edges of pastry in the dish. Place second sheet of pastry on top and pinch edges with bottom pastry to seal, like a pie crust. Brush with egg wash.

Bake dish for 1 hour until dark golden brown. Cool at least 15 minutes before serving.

My brother in law, KC, is very hard to please on the food front. He likes everything plain with only salt and pepper, steaks cooked dry almost burnt, plain rice. I have tried over the last couple of years to change his food attitude and have succeeded with some dishes. He likes my chili, spaghetti, beef vegetable soup, enchiladas and my fresh made basil pesto with noodles. So we are progressing. He is actually eating things he would never eat. I recently made a simple chicken dish that he really liked so here it is.

SMOKEY CHICKEN CORDON BLEU

4 Large boneless, skinless chicken breast, split in halves and pounded thin
8 Slices thin prosciutto ham
8 Thin slices smoked Gouda cheese, cut each slice in half making 16 pieces
1 Cup Italian bread crumbs
½ Cup Panko bread crumbs
1 Stick of Butter melted
Salt and pepper
Paprika

Heat the oven to 375 degrees. Spray a baking dish with cooking spray.

Place breast halves in a plastic bag and pound with flat side of meat mallet. You should have 8 pieces. Lightly sprinkle salt and pepper on both sides of chicken pieces.

Mix Italian and Panko bread crumbs in a bowl. Place melted butter in second bowl.

Place one piece prosciutto ham on chicken and two half pieces of cheese to cover most of ham. Starting from one end, roll chicken into jelly roll. You can secure it with toothpicks if you like. Dip roll in butter and then in bread crumbs to coat. Place in baking dish seam side down and repeat until all 8 are finished. Lightly sprinkle with Paprika and any butter that's left. Bake until brown and crispy. This should take about 30 minutes, but you should test inside temperature to see if it has reached 165 degrees.

Our fresh market, Sprouts, has thin sliced Smoked Gouda. If yours doesn't, ask your deli to slice it for you.

Sis and I love lobster. We like it cooked all different ways, especially lobster bisque. I have had lobster mac and cheese but couldn't taste the lobster flavor until I bit into a piece of lobster meat. So one day, I decided to make some lobster mac and cheese. I wanted the full flavor of the lobster throughout the dish. I started with a small amount of bisque and incorporated it into the mac and cheese with the lobster meat. It was really good. I only made a small amount since KC doesn't like lobster and it is expensive. Kay and I had some and decided to go out shopping. While we shopped, we mentioned that we would have the rest of the lobster mac and cheese when we got home. You know how hungry you get shopping for food and we were starving. After getting home and putting away the groceries, we decided to relax and have our mac and cheese. It wasn't there. We looked everywhere in the refrigerator and even checked the freezer to see if I absent mindedly put it in there. Nope, not there. So Kay asked KC if he had something to eat. He said he didn't know what it was, but it was good and he ate it all. What the?!!! He still doesn't like lobster and he really doesn't care for my home made mac and cheese as he prefers the gooey kind in a box. So you can bet your lobster shells, I label and freeze any leftovers!!!

I have made Lobster Mac and Cheese several times with different ingredients trying to get the best lobster flavor with a creamy mac and cheese. I tried a smoky cheese, but it hid the lobster flavor and I added this and that and took it back out. So this was my best attempt, a creamy mac and cheese made with a flavorful stock and lots of lobster.

LOBSTER BISQUE MAC AND CHEESE

6 Lobster tails 4oz. each, raw, split and meat removed cut in pieces, shells in a pot for stock
8 oz. Farfalle pasta
2 Tablespoons fine chopped onion
2 Tablespoons fine chopped celery
1 Clove of garlic minced
2 oz. Cream cheese cut into cubes
8 Tablespoons butter
2 Tablespoons self-rising flour
½ Cup heavy cream or ½ and ½
1 Cup Gruyere cheese, shredded
1 Cup Monterey Jack cheese, shredded
1 Cup Sharp Cheddar cheese, shredded
1 Cup Breton original crackers, crushed, or Ritz
¼ Teaspoon salt
½ Teaspoon pepper
¼ Teaspoon Paprika
1/8 each Nutmeg and Cayenne pepper

To shells in pot, add just enough water to cover and salt, onion, celery, and garlic. Bring to boil, reduce heat and simmer until liquid is reduced to about a cup or cup and a half of stock. This will take 20 to 30 minutes.

Boil pasta according to box directions. Drain and set aside covered. Preheat oven 350 degrees

Melt 4 tablespoons butter in sauce pan, medium heat. Add lobster pieces and sauté until just done. Don't overcook. Remove half of pieces to a cutting surface and chop into small pieces. Add this along with larger pieces in butter into pot of pasta and stir, and then stir in cream cheese. Cover and let cream cheese soften, 10 minutes. Stir a little to blend. Cover.

Once stock is reduced and you have at least a cup, strain and measure 1 cup.

In medium pot, melt 2 tablespoons butter; add flour, pepper, cayenne pepper and nutmeg and paprika. Stir on low heat for 3 to 4 minutes until bubbly, add cup of stock and stir until it thickens. Remove from heat and add cream and stir until smooth. Add cheeses and stir. Return to heat and stir until smooth, but cheese doesn't have to be fully melted. Empty into pasta and stir to blend well.

Spray 9x9 baking dish with cooking spray. Add pasta mixture.

Melt 2 tablespoons butter and stir into cracker crumbs. I know, more butter. But if you're gonna have lobster mac and cheese once a year, forget about the butter and just enjoy. Take up jogging for a couple of months. Top mac and cheese with crumbs. Bake in oven for 40 minutes until bubbly and there is a brown crust on edges and cracker crumbs have browned. Remove and cool at least 10 minutes.

There is no way to make this dish lean AND wonderful, so just eat it.

Whew! Time to lighten it up a bit after that heavy mac and cheese. My friend Judy and I really like to go out for Thai food. It's spicy and fresh and has great flavor. So when I thought of making a Thai dish, I thought of Lettuce Wraps. They are light and full of flavor and crunch.

LETTUCE WRAPS

1 Pound ground pork-you may use ground turkey but you sacrifice flavor
3 Green scallions, thinly sliced
1 Medium carrot, shredded
15 Snow pea pods, string removed and sliced cross ways
1 Tablespoon fresh grated ginger
2 Tablespoons Soy sauce, low sodium
2 Tablespoons Thai peanut sauce
1 Tablespoon Szechuan hot and spicy marinade sauce
3 Tablespoons chopped peanuts
2 Tablespoons chopped fresh cilantro leaves
½ Tablespoon fresh lime juice
2 Large cloves of garlic, pressed in garlic press
Ice Berge lettuce leaves

In a medium fry pan, cook ground pork over medium heat until done; add green onions, ginger, soy sauce, peanut sauce, Szechuan sauce, and garlic. Cook, stirring, until pork is well mixed and flavored by all the ingredients, about 5 minutes, then add the carrot, pea pods and peanuts. Stir to mix another 2 minutes. Remove from heat and stir in fresh cilantro and lime juice. Cool a few minutes before serving in lettuce leaves.

I like to mix a small amount of wasabi with soy sauce to drizzle on top. It's very spicy.

Even though we don't have the east coast delicacies here on the west coast, we do have fresh wild caught Alaskan Salmon. It is so fresh and succulent and healthy and it is great any way it's prepared. Recently, I was invited to dinner at the home of a friend from ceramics class. It was a wonderful evening enjoying California's Almond Champagne and wonderful food Geraldine prepared. One dish was marinated Salmon. I told her it reminded me of a dish Jim and I enjoyed on the Outer Banks, marinated Blue fish. Most people don't like Blue fish as it is oily, but we would go to the surf fishermen in the freezing cold and get the small ones since they were less oily than the larger. Jim would clean them immediately making sure to remove the dark bloody meat that contained the oil. We would put it on ice and take it home and make a wonder dish. Since I can't get Blue fish, I thought I would try this dish with Salmon.

MARINATED SALMON

1 8 oz. portion fresh wild caught Salmon, boneless and skinless, cut into bite size pieces
2 Tablespoons butter
Juice of 2 limes
Juice of 1 lemon
Pinch of salt, pepper, paprika
¼ Cup of cracker crumbs like Ritz mixed with a tablespoon of melted butter

In medium pot, heat butter until melted, add lime and lemon juice, salt, pepper, and paprika. Bring to simmer. Remove from heat and stir in salmon, cover and let marinate for 30 minutes, stirring once or twice to make sure all of salmon is mixed in juices.

Heat the oven to 375. Spray small oven safe bowl with cooking spray. Using slotted spoon, transfer salmon from pot to bowl draining off most of juices. Top with cracker crumbs. Bake 10 minutes and then turn oven to broil. Broil until cracker crumbs are browned. Serve warm.

This is enough for two as a snack or a meal if you add a small salad and/or pasta. When I made this, I also made the fresh Alfredo sauce with pasta. Sis added her salmon to her pasta and loved the flavors. I added my portion to the top of my salad.

Ok, I'm almost done. Are you jumping up and down and happy? I am. I really love all foods; I just can't put everything I love in this book. I would be in my coffin with hands clutching my lap top.

I'm not much of a baker. I will make a cake preferably cheese cake or just a plain yellow cake for Sis as she is not much of a chocolate fan. I know, right? That's a deal breaker as you know I love chocolate. I've failed miserably trying to make bread, so I leave the bread baking to my neighbor and friend, Greg. He makes wonderful breads and hand delivers right out of the oven. Bet you wish you had a neighbor like that! And did I mention, he is a great cook and I feel a little humbled around him. So when he invited us to a patio party, I decided to bake a chocolate cake. My daughter, Renee, gave me this recipe and it is the best and Greg liked it. So, this one is for you Greg for all the wonderful breads you so generously give.

TEXAS SHEET CAKE

In a 2 quart sauce pan combine:
1 Cup of butter
4 Heaping tablespoons Cocoa
1 Cup of water

Heat to boiling-remove and add:
2 Cups flour
2 Cups sugar
½ Teaspoon salt

Beat until mixed and add:
½ Cup sour cream
1 Teaspoon baking soda
2 Eggs slightly beaten

Blend and pour into a greased and floured sheet pan 15 x 1 ½ inches. Bake 375 degrees for 20 minutes. Test middle with tooth pick.

While cake is cooling, in another sauce pan,

Bring to boil:
½ Cup of butter
6 Tablespoons milk
4 Tablespoons Cocoa

Remove and add:
1 Box 1 pound powdered sugar
1 Teaspoon vanilla extract
1 Cup chopped pecans

Stir to blend and spread over cake. Cool if you can wait that long or eat a piece like I do while it is still warm. OMG! Scrumdiddlyumptious.

Well, I saved the best for last. My best loved food in California second to wine. I've told you about how much I love fish and shrimp tacos because of the fresh ingredients and taste. California is known for fish tacos. After all they originated just south of us in Mexico. My sister introduced me to them many years ago and I've enjoyed them each time I visited and have fallen in love with them over the years. I enjoy going to Rubio's for a fish taco fix, but also enjoy making my own. Casey Michael, my nephew and one of my partners in Dragon's Breath Salsa also loves fish tacos. I blacken, grill, or fry the fish. Any way you cook it is great. It's the fresh ingredients that make them special, fresh cabbage, fresh Pico De Gallo, cilantro, fresh salsas. Yummy goodness. You can use any fresh fish; I like wild caught Cod because it is firm and not fishy tasting. Mahi, Mahi with mango and habanero salsa is delicious. I like my chili lime grilled shrimp tacos as well. Let your creative juices flow.

FISH OR SHRIMP TACOS

Use the Beer Batter recipe for frying fish. You can substitute Old Bay seasoning with a mild taco seasoning which I also use for blackening or grilling.

1 Pound Cod, cut into pieces that will fit nicely into a taco size tortilla, about 8 pieces
8 Corn or flour taco size tortillas
2 Cups finely shredded cabbage
Fresh Pico De Gallo, use recipe in this book
Fresh lime wedges
Any fresh salsa you like or make your own

Fresh sauce with Sriracha:

1 Cup sour cream
½ Cup mayonnaise
1/8 Teaspoon salt
¼ Teaspoon pepper
Juice of two limes
Zest of one lime
1 Teaspoon dried or fresh chopped dill weed
1 Bunch fresh cilantro, stems removed and leaves chopped
3 Teaspoons Sriracha hot sauce, more if you like it hotter

Mix all ingredients, refrigerate a few hours for flavors to blend.

Dip fish pieces in beer batter and deep fry 375 degrees until golden brown. Drain on paper towels until you are ready to build your taco.

GRILLED CHILI LIME SHRIMP

1 Pound large-21/25 count-shrimp, peeled, deveined, rinsed and patted dry
2 Large cloves garlic, pressed in garlic press
½ Cup chopped fresh cilantro leaves
Juice of 1 lime
3 Tablespoons of melted butter
¼ Teaspoon taco seasoning
Grilling skewers

In medium bowl, combine garlic, cilantro, lime juice, taco seasoning and melted butter. Add shrimp and mix until coated.

Place shrimp on skewers, just enough to fit flat on grill. Grill on high only about two minutes on each side. Shrimp can over cook quickly. Remove from grill and slide shrimp off skewers into bowl ready to build your tacos.

At this point, it is as simple as choosing which taco tortilla you like, corn or flour. I usually heat it quickly in a pan, turning once, long enough to just heat it and not dry out.

Use fish or shrimp and add whatever toppings you like.

My mouth is watering so I think I'll call Casey, cook some tacos, sit on the back patio and celebrate *life.*

Well, that's it in a nut shell and yes I have been called nut many times, but it's **O K.**

It's Just Me!

Printed in the United States
By Bookmasters